The Eat-less-meat Book: War Ration Cookery...

Mrs. C. S. Peel

WAR RATION COOKERY
(THE EAT-LESS-MEAT BOOK)

THE EAT-LESS-MEAT BOOK

WAR RATION COOKERY

NEW EDITION, REVISED

BY

MRS. C. S. PEEL

*Co-Director of Women's Service, Ministry of
Food, during the Economy Campaign*

AUTHOR OF

" 10S. A HEAD FOR HOUSE BOOKS
(*Revised Edition*)
" LEARNING TO COOK," ETC. ETC.

LONDON: JOHN LANE, THE BODLEY HEAD
NEW YORK: JOHN LANE COMPANY: MCMXVIII

Third Edition, revised to meet present
conditions

PRINTED AT THE COMPLETE PRESS, WEST NORWOOD, S.E.

PREFACE

THE greater part of this book appeared in *The Queen* and in the *Daily Mail*. My thanks are due to the editors of those newspapers for permission to republish them.

I do not claim originality for these recipes (though I believe that some of them have never appeared in print before), but I do claim that they are freed of unnecessary materials which cost money, of unnecessary processes which absorb valuable time, and that they are economical of the foods most difficult to obtain. I hope also that they are so worded that, if needs be, inexperienced persons can work from them. They have now been revised for the third time to meet present-day conditions.

DOROTHY C. PEEL

NOTE

Owing to war conditions, prices and stocks of food vary so much from week to week that the housekeeper must avail herself of the state of the market and make use of those recipes the ingredients of which happen to be procurable at the moment.

CONTENTS

I

WAR RATION HOUSEKEEPING

IMPORTANT NOTE

The sale of cream is now illegal. Butter and margarine should not be used for cooking : substitute any clarified fat, including cocoa butter, which needs to be twice clarified to eliminate the taste of cocoa.

Dried eggs may be used instead of fresh.

Custard powder is a good substitute for fresh egg custard.

Egg powder has little nourishing value but is useful in many cases.

When the recipe mentions milk, half milk and half water may be substituted or tinned milk (unsweetened) can be used.

" Of our men we ask their lives, their limbs—
of ourselves a little less food "

I
WAR RATION HOUSEKEEPING

I DO not write this book from the point of view of the food reformer (though I think the diet of both rich and poor needs reform), neither do I write as a vegetarian (though I sympathize with many of their views), but I do write it hoping that I may thereby help those who have a difficult task to feed their households sufficiently and yet are loyally trying to do their duty to their country.

When the food supply is limited it is more than ever necessary that the best use should be made of available material, and only by a great and united effort can we ensure that the rising generation and the generation about to be born shall receive sufficient nourishment in the months ahead of us.

The Meat Question

To judge by the letters which have appeared in the daily press and from private conversations it would seem that many people imagine that to abstain from meat on several days of the week will seriously affect their health. But vast numbers of people appear able to live quite healthily without any meat at all, and there seems good reason to believe that the well-to-do of this nation have suffered in health in pre-war days from eating too great a quantity of meat.

The persons who are so distressed that they cannot obtain what they consider a sufficient quantity of meat do not realize perhaps that in numbers of working-class families the women and children have never eaten meat more than once or twice a week, the greater part of the small supply of meat which could be afforded being eaten by the husband and father, who as wage-earner was the person most to be considered.

But when meat is very scarce, other suitable foods must of course be substituted. The best substitutes for meat are the fatty fishes (that is salmon, herrings, fresh and cured, eels, mackerel, sprats, sardines), eggs, cheese, and nuts, which contain protein and fat. Pulses contain protein, but do not contain fat and need the addition of that necessary item of diet.

The Rise in Prices

It is very difficult to obtain any correct information as to the rise in the cost of living. Prices fluctuate, also if one material is unobtainable at the moment another which, perhaps, is dearer must be substituted, but, roughly, I think the town housekeeper must count that the cost of food has now doubled.

Those folk who have their own garden and farm produce do not suffer so much from high prices, because they can preserve eggs, fruit, and vegetables when plentiful, and so level up the cost of the year's living, and although pig and poultry food, garden requisites, and labour are " up," the producer saves the wholesale and retail profits and cost of distribution, which add quite 100 per cent. to the town customer's bill. But putting aside these favoured persons, and allowing for the prices which obtain in large towns, the housekeeper, *if she lived in the style possible on a 10s. a head pre-war allowance*, would now have to spend practically £1 per head.

Needless to say, persons whose income never allowed of any but a small surplus, and who have also to meet increased taxation, as well as an increase in the total cost of living (clothing, wages, washing, fuel, light, etc.), cannot possibly afford for each person some 18s. worth of food per week (omitting the cost of cleaning materials), so they are obliged *to cut down their standard of living*.

What must we Eat? and How much must we Eat?

The questions which now present themselves are, *What amount of food per day is necessary to keep people in health?* and *What kind of food must it be?* These questions are not easy to answer, for even the great authorities differ in their conclusions. The average reader will have neither the time nor perhaps the desire to study the many scientific works which have been written on diet, nor is it necessary that he should, because we take it for granted here that he is not proposing to become a vegetarian, or even a non-meat eater, but that he desires merely to adopt a diet containing less meat, fat, and sugar than he formerly consumed, and to substitute to some degree cheap for costly foods, and it becomes quite evident from a study of the following budgets that even if we eat far less meat, making up with other though no less nourishing foods, our health need not suffer.

In *Poverty, A Study of Town Life*, by Seebohm Rowntree, the author, after most careful inquiry into the conditions of life amongst the poor in York (and Mr. Charles Booth in his *Life and Labour of the People in London* seems to arrive at similar conclusions), is of the opinion that " (1) *The diet of the middle classes is generally more than adequate*; (2) that of the well-to-do artisan is on the whole adequate; but (3) that of the labouring class is seriously inadequate."

Many interesting budgets are given in *Poverty*, amongst others those of some middle-class (servant-keeping) families. Here, for example, is one :

B

Budget No. 23.   Six Adults and Three Children

List of Food-stuffs used during Week ending
June 10, 1901

2lb. currants, 1s. ; 6oz. raisins, 4d. ; 1¾ stone flour, 2s. 6d. ; yeast, 3d. ; 7lb. moist sugar, 1s. 5½d. ; 11lb. loaf sugar, 2s. 3d. ; 1 tin Neave's food, 8½d. ; 4lb. butter, 4s. ; 1lb. cheese, 8d. ; 1lb. tea, 2s. ; 5lb. fresh haddock, 2s. 6d. ; ½lb. cocoa, 1s. 5d. ; 1lb. coffee, 1s. 4d. ; 2lb. biscuits, 1s. 4d. ; 1 tin sardines, 1s. 3d. ; 2 rabbits, 2s. 6d. ; 2 stone potatoes, 1s. 6d. ; 8lb. green gooseberries, 2s. 6d. ; 30 eggs, 2s. ; ½ lb. rice, 1½d. ; 15lb. marmalade, 3s. 9d. ; 16lb. sirloin beef, 13s. ; 3½ lb. beefsteak, 3s. 6d. ; cauliflower, 3d. ; tea cakes, 8d. ; 9lb. bacon, 5s. 8d. ; 1½ lb. salmon, 2s. 6d. ; 2lb. jam, 8d. ; 2lb. tomatoes, 1s. 4d. ; lettuce, 10d. ; ½lb. sponge cakes, 4d. ; 8½ lb. mutton, 7s. ; 1 tin sardines, 1s. 4d. ; 2lb. chicken and tongue, 2s. 6d.

Menu of Meals provided during Week ending
June 10, 1901

FRIDAY.—*Breakfast :* Fish cakes, sardines, fried bacon, bread, butter, marmalade, tea, coffee. *Dinner :* Rabbits, potatoes, gooseberry tart, rice pudding, cream, sugar. *Tea :* Bread, butter, jam, cakes, tea. *Supper :* Cheese, biscuits, bread, butter, cakes, cocoa.

SATURDAY.—*Breakfast :* Fish, sardines, fried bacon, bread, butter, marmalade, tea, coffee. *Dinner :* Beefsteak, potatoes, cauliflower, queen of puddings, rice pudding, cream. *Tea :* Bread, butter, marmalade, cakes, tea. *Supper :* Cheese, biscuits, bread, butter, cakes, cocoa, milk, coffee.

SUNDAY.—*Breakfast :* Bacon, poached eggs, bread, butter, marmalade, tea, coffee. *Dinner :* Roast beef, Yorkshire pudding, roast potatoes, rice pudding, gooseberry tart, cream, sugar. *Tea :* Bread, butter, jam, cakes, tea. *Supper :* Cheese, biscuits, bread, butter, cake, cocoa, milk.

MONDAY.—*Breakfast :* Bacon, sardines, bread, butter, marmalade, tea, coffee. *Dinner :* Cold beef, salad, potatoes, sponge cake, custard pudding, rice. *Tea :* Bread, butter, cakes, marmalade, tea. *Supper :* Eggs, biscuits, bread, butter, cakes, cocoa, milk.

TUESDAY. — *Breakfast :* Fried bacon, poached eggs, bread, butter, marmalade, tea, coffee. *Dinner :* Cold beef, salad, hashed beef, potatoes, stewed fruit, rice pudding. *Tea :* Bread, butter, cakes, marmalade, tea. *Supper :* Cheese, biscuits, bread, butter, cakes, cocoa, coffee, milk.

WEDNESDAY.—*Breakfast :* Fried bacon, sardines, bread, butter, marmalade, tea, coffee. *Dinner :* Roast mutton, jelly, potatoes, cabbage, gooseberry tart, pancakes. *Tea :* Bread, butter, cakes, jam, marmalade, tea. *Supper :* Cheese, biscuits, bread, butter, cakes, cocoa, milk.

T H U R S D A Y.—*Breakfast :* Chicken and tongue mould, bread, butter, marmalade, tea, coffee. *Dinner :* Cold mutton, potatoes, salad, curry, rice pudding, stewed fruit. *Tea :* Bread, butter, cakes, jam, marmalade, tea. *Supper :* Cheese, biscuits, bread, butter, cakes, cocoa, milk.

The total cost of food *at pre-war prices* is £3 14s. 0½d., and if instead of supper we add late dinner for three or four adults, that would certainly increase the food bill to 10s. a head, or at present nearly £1 per head per week, *for food only.* Yet this diet, even if late dinner of simple kind is added, would not have been considered at all unusual in a well-to-do middle-class household before the year 1914.

In rich households it is improbable that more food would have been consumed (when we allow for late dinner), but it would be of a more varied and more costly kind with extravagant adjuncts.

Let us now compare the bill of fare No. 23 with two of Mr. Rowntree's labourer's budgets, and at the same time let us bear in mind these facts : A man or woman doing hard physical labour requires more food than one leading a sedentary life. Now the labourer and the working woman are generally doing hard or moderately hard physical work (the woman does her own scrubbing, cleaning, cooking, etc.), and the children frequently do household tasks or other work before and after going to school. Therefore, speaking generally, the working-class family need more food than do the well-to-do family, and they obtain far less.

Budget No. 7. Carter. Wages (Regular) 20s.

The father drives a lorry ; he is now in regular work, but was out of work for six months last year. During that period the family incurred a heavy debt, which Mrs. D.

is now striving to clear off. Questioned as to how they lived during these six months, when Mr. D. was earning no regular money, Mrs. D. replied that she did not know; her brother was very kind to her and bought shoes for herself and the children, her mother gave her odd things, and for the rest they got into debt.

There are two children, a boy aged 5, and a little girl aged 2.

The budget was kept for eight consecutive weeks during February and March 1901. The total income during this period was £8 14s. 6d. Mr. D. made some overtime, and Mrs. D. was also able to earn a little money.

The deficiency in the energy value of the diet amounts to ·5 per cent., that of the protein supply to 18 per cent.

Purchases during Week ending
February 22, 1901

FRIDAY.—2 bags of coal, 2s. 6d.; 1½ stone flour, 2s.; yeast, 1d.; 4lb. sugar, 7d.; ¼lb. tea, 4½d.; 1lb. butter, 1s.; 3½lb.

bacon, 1s. 5d. ; firewood, 2d. ; ½lb. lard, 2½d.; baking powder, 1d. ; 6 eggs, 6d. ; candles, 1d. ; matches, ½d. ; 1lb. soap, 2d. ; starch, 1d. ; soda, 1d.

SATURDAY.—Doctor's bill, 1s. 3d. ; frying-pan, 6½d. ; 2 teaspoons, 1d. ; 1 tablespoon, 2d. ; ½ stone potatoes, 5d. ; cabbage, 2d. ; 3lb. pork, 1s. 7½d. ; 1lb. onions, 1d. ; 1 quart oil, 2½d. ; ½lb. rice, 1d. ; milk, 1d. ; ¼lb. coffee, 3d. ; kippers, 2d. ; 2 tins condensed milk, 5d.

MONDAY.—Insurance, 11d. ; club, 1s. 3d. ; doctor's bill, 1s.

TUESDAY.—Debt, 1s. ; 1lb. figs, 5d.

Menu of Meals provided during Week ending February 22, 1901

FRIDAY.—*Breakfast :* Bread, butter, tea. *Dinner :* Bread, butter, toast, tea. *Tea :* Bread, butter, tea.

SATURDAY.—*Breakfast :* Bread, bacon, coffee. *Dinner :* Bacon, potatoes, pudding, tea. *Tea :* Bread, butter, shortcake, tea. *Supper :* Tea, bread, kippers.

SUNDAY.—*Breakfast :* Bread, butter, shortcake, coffee. *Dinner :* Pork, onions, potatoes, Yorkshire pudding. *Tea :* Bread, butter, shortcake, tea. *Supper :* Bread and meat.

MONDAY.—*Breakfast :* Bread, bacon, butter, tea. *Dinner :* Pork, potatoes, pudding, tea. *Tea :* Bread, butter, tea. *Supper :* One cup of tea.

TUESDAY.—*Breakfast :* Bread, bacon, butter, coffee. *Dinner :* Pork, bread, tea. *Tea :* Bread, butter, boiled eggs, tea. *Supper :* Bread, butter, bacon, tea.

WEDNESDAY.—*Breakfast :* Bread, bacon, butter, tea. *Dinner :* Bacon and eggs, potatoes, bread, tea. *Tea :* Bread, butter, tea.

THURSDAY.—*Breakfast :* Bread, butter, coffee. *Dinner :* Bread, bacon, tea. *Tea :* Bread, butter, tea.

Budget No. 9. Labourer. Wages 18s.

The household consists of a father, aged 27, and mother, aged 22, and a baby 10 months old.

There is a deficiency of 38 per cent. of protein in this family's diet, and of 29 per cent. in its fuel value.

Purchases during Week ending April 26, 1901

FRIDAY.—½ stone flour, 7½d. ; yeast, 1d. ; ¼ lb. tea, 7½d. ; 2lb. sugar, 4d. ; ½lb. butter, 6d. ; ¼lb. cocoa, 2d. ; 2 candles, 2½d. ; 2 pints milk, 3d. ; ½lb. currants, 2d. ; tablet of soap, 1½d. ; 1lb. soap, 3d.

SATURDAY.—2½lb. bacon, 1s. 6d. ; 1lb. sausage, 6d. ; 2lb. beef, 1s. ; kettle, 6½d. ; 2 pints milk, 3d. ; bowl, 6½d. ; hat for baby, 11d. ; 2 bags of coal, 3s. ; 1 tin Neave's food, 7½d. ; ½ stone potatoes, 3½d. ; two tea cakes, 1½d.

SUNDAY.—2 pints milk, 3d.

MONDAY.—Rent, 3s. 3d. ; back rent, 3s.

TUESDAY.—2 pints milk, 3d.

WEDNESDAY.—2 pints milk, 3d.

THURSDAY.—Loaf of bread, 3d. ; 2 pints milk, 3d. ; 1 pint paraffin, 1½d.

Menu of Meals provided during Week ending April 26, 1901

FRIDAY.—*Breakfast :* Bread, cheese, tea. *Dinner :* Potatoes, bread, tea. *Tea :* Bread, butter, tea.

SATURDAY. — *Breakfast :* " Dip," bread, butter, tea. *Dinner :* Sausages, bread. *Tea :* Bread, cocoa, jam, tea.

SUNDAY.—*Breakfast :* Bacon, bread, toast, tea. *Dinner :* Meat, potatoes, Yorkshire pudding. *Tea :* Bread, pie, tea cakes, tea.

MONDAY.—*Breakfast :* Bacon, bread, tea. *Dinner :* Bacon, bread, tea. *Tea :* Bacon, bread, tea.

TUESDAY.—*Breakfast :* Bread, meat, tea, *Dinner :* Meat, bread, tea. *Tea :* Meat, bread, tea.

WEDNESDAY.—*Breakfast :* Bacon, bread, tea. *Dinner :* Meat, bread, tea. *Tea :* Eggs, " dip," bread, tea.

THURSDAY.—*Breakfast :* Bread, butter, tea. *Dinner :* Meat, bread, " dip," tea. *Tea :* Meat, bread, butter, tea.

The two budgets quoted may be called good and bad, No. 7 being that of a good, and No. 9 that of a bad manager; but in neither case does the food provide a sufficiency of nourishment.

The cost of No. 7 at pre-war price is 9s. 11½d. for food; at the present time it would be about 18s. to 19s.

The cost of No. 9 at pre-war price is 7s. 9½d. for food; at the present time it would be about 14s. to 15s.

FOOD VALUES

When calculating the deficiency of energy value and protein in the working-class budgets given by him in *Poverty*, Mr. Rowntree takes as the standard for a man doing " moderate " work, 3500 calories; doing severe work, 4500 calories; doing light work, 3000 calories; without muscular work, 2700 calories; and allows for women and children, taking the man's food as the unit : Women, 80 per cent.; boy, 14 to 16, 80 per cent.; girl, 14 to 16, 70 per cent.; child, 10 to 13, 60 per cent.; child, 6 to 9, 50 per cent.; child, 2 to 5, 40 per cent.; under 2, 30 per cent. Some authorities consider this too high a standard.

Speaking humbly as a mother and a housekeeper, and after consultation with other mothers, it seems to me that the amount of food allowed for children over six is too small and that boys at all events of 9 eat quite as much as a woman, and those of

14 and upwards practically as much as a man.

A calorie is a unit of heat. A man requires, to enable him to do " moderate " physical work, sufficient food to produce 3500 calories of heat per day, and " our requirements in food can be stated in calories, or in ' fuel value ' . . . because food resembles fuel; and the value of what we eat can be measured by the amount of heat it can produce in the body " (*Food Values*, by M. McKillop, M.A.). " No one article of food contains the different nutritive constituents in proper proportion " (*Food and the Principles of Dietetics*, by Robert Hutchinson). Therefore we have to live on a varied diet in order to obtain the necessary nutriment we require. To put the matter briefly, we need body-building and repairing foods, heat and energy foods, mineral and ballast foods, water, and some spices and condiments. The three former (roughly) are :

1. Fish, lean meat, eggs, cheese, nuts, pulses, or legumens.
2. Starches, sugars, fats.
3. Vegetables and fruits.

Now let us put into ordinary housekeeping language some of the terms used by food experts.

PROTEIN. — Protein is chiefly present in the body-building foods; sugar contains none; the starchy preparations contain practically none; and the same may be said of most purified fats and oils.

The Foods we Eat

We are often advised to substitute *pulses* or *legumens* for meat, but many people are rather vague as to the foods to which these names apply. The following foods are pulses or legumens: Peas (fresh and dried); beans (haricots, butter, broad, kidney); lentils (Egyptian or red and the brown lentil).

What, then, are cereals? Wheat, barley, maize (or Indian corn), oats, rice; and the various preparations made with wheaten flour, such as macaroni, vermicelli, spaghetti, semolina, farina. Oats (oatmeal, groats). Barley (pearl barley; pot barley, roughly ground; patent barley, crushed to the state of flour; barley meal, the whole grain ground into meal). Maize or Indian corn (hominy, cornflour, tinned sweet corn, Indian meal, etc.). Sago (the pith of the sago palm ; sold as pearl, medium, or bullet). Tapioca (obtained from the root of the tapioca plant, and sold in various sizes).

If to all the pulses and cereals we add fruit, vegetables, and nuts, cheese, milk, butter, and fats (the latter are, of course, animal foods), it is evident that we can of necessity enjoy a very satisfying and varied diet without the aid of the more costly meat, fish, and eggs, though a limited use of the latter certainly lightens the difficulties of the caterer's task.

And now a word on

Cooking

I never tire of saying that there are only two kinds of cooking—

Bad Cooking and Good Cooking

People talk about plain cooking and high-class cooking, but the fact remains that if you can cook you can cook !

People cook badly because often—I may say generally—they have not been taught the groundwork of the business, and their ignorance of cause and effect hampers them. But any person of average intelligence who is willing to take pains, if able to obtain good teaching, could certainly learn to cook well in six weeks to three months. I say this quite aware that most cooks will disagree with me, and nevertheless I say it again.

An intelligent, painstaking person after a few weeks of *scientific* teaching and personal experiment could cook well, and what more she wanted to know she could learn from books and experiment. But, alas, English-women are seldom taught to cook or to realize that a cook is as valuable—more valuable, indeed—to her country than many a better-paid and more highly esteemed person.

In the following recipes I have tried to explain clearly and minutely how the dishes mentioned are prepared—taking it for granted that the person who is cooking is inexperienced. Armed with these recipes and the desire to carry them out faithfully, I doubt if any one can go far wrong in their preparation. But in fairness to the cook who has not a great deal of time to give to actual cooking, let me warn the mistress that meatless dishes do as a rule take considerably more time to cook than is required by the joint and plain pudding style of diet, and it is only fair to make allowance for this fact.

Food Values

Those of my readers who have a taste for arithmetic and time to devote to it can calculate the food value of any recipe given by the help of *Food Values and How to Calculate Them,* by M. McKillop, M.A.

II
STOCKS AND SOUPS

NOTE

*Some of these recipes might be made cheaper
by omitting egg and milk, but as soups nowadays often take the place of meat they need to
be specially nourishing.*

II

STOCKS AND SOUPS

OF all aids to economical cooking soup is, I think, the greatest, because it may be made from material which it would be difficult to use for home consumption in any other way. Also after consuming a portion of nourishing soup considerably less of other and more expensive food is needed. The idea that soup cannot be made without soup meat or bones has had, perforce, to die, though the old-fashioned or inexperienced cook may still be heard to murmur, " Soup ? But there is nothing to make it of." Let us see, then, what we need for soup-making, cutting out of our list any which cannot be termed War Soups.

The stock needed for everyday use, and generally termed

Second Stock (Semi-Meatless)

is made thus : Take any cooked bones or raw bones that you may have, game or poultry carcases, trimmings of meat, skin and gristle, and break them into small pieces. Remove the marrow of large bones and add this to your supply of fat. It will spoil the stock and make it cloudy. Allow about 1lb. of bones to one quart of cold water. Bring slowly to the boil, skim, simmer two hours. Now to each quart of water add one sliced and cleaned carrot, turnip, onion, the root and green tops, and, if necessary, outside leaves of some celery, two or three parsley stalks, some herbs, and two cloves tied in muslin, four peppercorns, and a pinch of salt and a pinch of sugar. If celery is not available, use a teaspoonful of celery seed tied in muslin. Simmer the contents of the pan for about one hour, and do bear in mind that boiling and simmering are not the same thing, and that if you boil when directed to simmer the result will be different. Simmering is cooking very gently, while boiling needs a heat of 212 degrees. If you boil this stock it will be cloudy and taste gluey. When the simmering is done, strain the soup into a basin and let it stand all night. Any fat there may be will now have formed in a solid cake. This fat is most valuable, and should be clarified and put away in a clean basin. The stock which results can then be used for any purpose for which stock is required (and there are many), and if a clear soup is needed quite a good one may be made thus :

A Cheap Clear Soup

To three pints of stock entirely cleared of fat add 1lb. of vegetables as before, twelve peppercorns, four allspice, two cloves, a portion of a blade of mace, and a pinch of sugar, the whisked white of an egg and the well-washed, crushed shell. Whisk over the fire until the soup nearly boils. Then remove the whisk and let the soup boil, and then simmer very gently for twenty minutes, and, lastly, strain through a clean cloth which has been wrung out in boiling water. Taste and add salt, pepper, and sugar to taste, and if the colour is not very good improve it with a teaspoonful of a vegetable extract called " marmite." Note that to succeed in obtaining a clear soup, the saucepan must be clean, the bones and vegetables thoroughly cleansed, the directions as to skimming, straining, and removing of fat carefully attended to. None of these directions are given for the pleasure of causing unnecessary trouble to the cook; they are given in order to achieve a required result.

The soup now only needs to be garnished and made very hot. But now let us go back to the materials. Our second stock was made from bones and vegetables. There is still something to be extracted from these. Add a fresh bone if you have it, and some vegetable trimmings, and some more seasoning, and repeat the proces of cooking as for the first stock, and so you have a well-flavoured second stock in which to cook beans, lentils, and savoury rice, or a foundation for sauce or thick soup. But do not forget that in hot weather stock which has vegetables in it will not keep well, and that all stock then should be boiled up once a day, and not kept longer than can be avoided.

But suppose it should happen that you have no bones of which to make soup? Well, you need not go soupless because of that.

But before I go on to describe the making of meatless stocks let me say a few words about bones. In many households the bones which could be used for soup and nourishing stock in which to cook meatless foods are thrown away off the plates.

For example, you have a rabbit and make a pie out of him—bones and all. But why not part cook him, take the meat for the pie, and reserve the bones for soup. Again, if you are a large family you may have a leg of mutton—serve it boned and stuffed and keep the raw bone for stock. Or you serve mutton cutlets—why not allow them to appear as noisettes and so save their valuable bones ?

But now to the consideration of meatless soups and stocks. The first recipe I give is one for a

Clear Vegetable Soup

which many people eat, fondly imagining it to be a *consommé* made with meat.

Ingredients.—1lb. mixed vegetables, twelve peppercorns, three cloves, one sprig of parsley, a teaspoonful of celery seed, salt and pepper, and a teaspoonful of " marmite "—

a vegetable extract bought in jars. *Method.*
—Thoroughly clean and slice the vegetables
and put them into a quart of cold water with
the peppercorns, cloves, parsley, celery seed
tied in muslin, salt and pepper. Bring to the
boil, and then simmer gently for three hours
and strain into a basin. When needed, add
a teaspoonful of marmite to each pint of
soup, and, if required, more seasoning, including a pinch of sugar and a suspicion of
honey. Serve very hot, with a garnish of
shred vegetables, macaroni, or prunes stewed
in stock and stoned and cut in half. Or
another nice and novel garnish consists of
well-washed tangerine orange-peel cut in
delicate shreds.

Two other clear soups may be made with
this foundation, namely—

Clear Tomato Soup

Squeeze from one or two ripe, sound, raw
tomatoes all the juice and strain it through
a clean cloth into the clear vegetable soup,
and simmer it for ten minutes before serving.
Taste to see if more salt, pepper, or sugar is
needed. Use the pulp for a savoury dish or
thick soup.

Clear Beetroot Soup

Proceed as before, using a teacupful of strained, cooked beetroot juice to each pint of soup, and garnish with shred beetroot. If the colour of these soups is not good it can be improved by using a drop or two of liquid carmine. The tomato soup should be quite pale coloured, the beetroot a dark red.

But I can hear some reader say, "This is all very well for people with gardens, but in towns vegetables are often exceedingly dear." Well, we cannot make even soup out of nothing, but we can use for it material (as I have already shown in the case of bones) that many people throw away. How many cooks would think of making stock out of vegetable peelings ? Yet a clear and well-tasting stock is the result of the following recipe if carefully carried out :

Stock Made from what is Generally Thrown Away

When peeling potatoes, onions, apples, pears, and using celery and parsley for other purposes, use the peelings and trimmings for stock. Before peeling, scrub and wash thoroughly, and then keep all the peel, **also** the cleansed root and green tops of the celery, ditto carrot, the stalks of parsley, the outside leaves (if clean and fresh) of lettuce, cabbage, cauliflower. Add water and seasoning, simmer and strain, and so make stock to use as a foundation for thick soup, or purée, or for cooking a meat roll in, or using as a foundation for sauce and savoury cereal and pulse dishes. The main point when making this soup is that the material used must be perfectly clean, and in no way decayed.

Vegetable Stock (Thick)

Ingredients.—Three-quarters of a pint of dried peas, two carrots, two onions, two cloves, a little celery (the green heads and roots and outside pieces), some parsley (and the stalks serve for this purpose), and ½oz. of margarine or clarified dripping, and salt.

Boil the peas (previously soaked overnight) for four hours in two and a half pints of water; they must be put into cold water. After the first boil, add every half-hour about a sherry-glass of cold water; this will help to soften the peas more thoroughly. After an hour and a half or two hours' time, add three carrots, two onions, three cloves, a little celery, some parsley, half a bay leaf, and the butter. Let the whole mixture simmer for five hours over a slow fire ; salt it moderately during the fourth hour, and strain off the vegetables when these are quite tender. This makes an excellent stock, and is very often used instead of meat stock for purées even in meat-eating households.

But often white soups are needed, and white stocks can be made for these as follows : *White Haricots.*—Soak the haricots overnight, and allow ½lb. to four quarts of cold water, stew gently for four hours, and strain. If the haricots are washed first the water they are soaked in can be used for cooking them in. *Rice.*—Allow ½lb. to four quarts of boiling water, and stew gently for one hour, and strain. *Macaroni.*—Allow ½lb. to four quarts of boiling water, and stew gently for one hour, and strain. *Pearl or Pot Barley.*—Allow ½lb. to four quarts of water, and stew gently for four hours, then strain. The barley can be used for some other purpose if not needed in the soup.

A White Soup (Made with Fish Stock)

Ingredients.—The water in which any washed fish has been boiled, milk (fresh or unsweetened condensed), salt, a pinch of curry powder, a little cornflour, a few spoonfuls of boiled rice. *Method.*—Boil the stock down until there is but half the quantity, then add an equal quantity of milk and water. Put in salt to taste, and then mix into half a cupful of the soup a pinch of curry powder and a spoonful of cornflour. Mix this smooth, and then stir it into the soup to make it of the consistency of cream. Put the boiled rice in the hot tureen and pour in the soup.

Economical Green Pea Soup

Ingredients.—One quart stock, half a pint of young green peas (measured after shelling), a few leaves of spinach and lettuce, 1oz. of fat, salt, sugar, and a little mint, flavouring. *Method.*—Wash and break up the pea shells, add the spinach and lettuce, wash and put into the boiling stock with a pinch of sugar, salt, and a little mint. Boil until the spinach, shells, and lettuce are soft, and pass through a fine sieve. Meanwhile cook the peas in the fat, a gill of boiling water, a little salt and sugar, shaking frequently until tender, pass through a fine sieve, add to the stock, colour with sap green, boil up, add a gill of milk, flavour and serve. This soup should be of the consistency of ordinary cream. Edgar's tinned marrowfats serve in winter, and it is difficult to detect that the soup has not been made with fresh peas. If liked, keep back a few whole peas to garnish with.

Celeriac Soup

Ingredients.—$\frac{1}{2}$ oz. fat, 3oz. sliced onion, 3oz. turnip, a root of celeriac (which has been well scraped and washed and cut into slices), two tablespoonfuls of rice flour, half a pint of milk, and one quart of stock, a small blade of mace, pinch of sugar, pepper and salt to taste. *Method.*—Melt the fat in a stewpan and add the onion, turnip, and celeriac. Cover the pan and let the vegetables simmer very gently for ten minutes, then stir in the rice flour (which has been previously mixed smoothly with milk), and the stock; continue to stir until the latter has boiled and thickened, then add the salt, pepper, sugar, and mace. Let the vegetables cook slowly until they are quite tender. Pass the soup and vegetables through a sieve and replace in the stewpan (which should first be rinsed), and mix by degrees with the pint of boiling milk. Let the soup simmer until it is required, but do not let it boil.

Purée of Lentils

Ingredients.—Half a pint yellow lentils, $\frac{1}{2}$ oz. clarified beef dripping, one onion, a sprig of parsley, thyme, and marjoram, one bay leaf, 1oz. flour, half a pint milk and water, pepper and salt, water. *Method.*—Soak the lentils in cold water for twelve hours. Wash them well. Place $\frac{1}{2}$oz. of fat in a casserole ; when it melts add to it an onion peeled and sliced, a sprig of parsley, thyme, and marjoram, and a bay leaf tied together. Fry for a few minutes, stirring all the time. Add the lentils and a quart of water, place the lid on, draw the pan to the side of the fire, and simmer gently for two hours. When all the vegetables are thoroughly cooked, rub them through a sieve into a clean sauce-

pan. Return to the fire. Mix 1oz. of barley
flour to a smooth paste by means of half a
wineglassful of cold milk. Place rather less
than half a pint of milk in a clean saucepan.
As soon as it boils, pour on to the mixed flour
and milk, return to the pan, and stir over
the fire until of the consistency of cream.
Add this to the soup by degrees, stirring all
the time, and continue to stir for five minutes.
Then add pepper and salt to taste, and
strain through a heated gravy strainer into
a hot soup tureen.

Tapioca Soup

Ingredients.—1oz. crushed tapioca, one
and a quarter pints of milk, two or three
sticks of celery, a turnip, one onion, two
cloves, one small bunch of parsley, one egg,
pepper and salt to taste. *Method.*—Wash the
tapioca in cold water and soak it for thirty
minutes, and put it into a saucepan containing one pint of boiling milk, which has
previously been boiled with the celery, turnip,
onion stock, with the two cloves and parsley,
and strained. Stir constantly until the
tapioca has swollen, and then leave it to

simmer, stirring it only occasionally. Whisk the yolk of one egg and mix it with a quarter of a pint of milk, and when the tapioca is thoroughly cooked pour it into the basin containing the egg, stir the soup well, add a seasoning of salt and pepper, and pour it back into the saucepan, and stir it over the fire for two or three minutes; the soup must not be allowed to boil after the egg is added or it will curdle.

Semolina Soup

Ingredients.—One quart of any of the white vegetable or cereal stocks, two tablespoon-fuls of semolina, half pint milk, salt, pepper. *Method.*—Put the stock on to boil, and when boiling sprinkle in the semolina, stirring well. Boil for ten minutes, add the milk and seasoning, reheat, and serve.

Chestnut Purée

Ingredients.—12oz. chestnuts, one onion, a stick of celery, a sprig of parsley, one quart of stock or water, half a pint of milk, pepper and salt to taste. *Method.*—Boil the chestnuts until all the skin can be removed.

Put them into a pan with one onion, the celery, parsley, and the stock or water. Simmer for an hour and a half, put through a sieve, then add the milk, return to the pan, bring to the boil, add some chopped parsley, pepper and salt. Make very hot and serve.

French Soup

A very Nutritious Soup for Children or Invalids

Ingredients.—One quart of milk, 1oz. of fat, two eggs, 1½ oz. flour. The milk should be flavoured with one small sliced onion and a little celery seed tied in muslin, or fresh celery if to hand, and a little parsley. Season to taste with salt and pepper. *Method.*— Melt the fat, add the flour, and stir to a smooth paste, then add the cool, flavoured milk gradually; when quite smooth let it boil, and then cool it slightly again. Add the yolks of two eggs well beaten; cook for three minutes, but do not let the soup boil. Pour the soup into a tureen and drop small spoonfuls of white of egg (beaten to a stiff froth) into the soup, and serve very hot.

D

A Cheap Vegetable Soup

Ingredients.—2lb. cabbage or sprouts, 2oz. fat, two quarts " peelings " stock, one dessertspoonful of cornflour, a little milk or water, salt, pepper, and seasoning to taste. *Method.*—Chop the cabbage or sprouts and fry slightly in the fat. Put this into a pan with the stock, pepper, salt, and seasoning. Boil, and then simmer for one hour and twenty minutes. Pass through a sieve, return to the pan, then add the cornflour previously mixed smooth with the water or milk. Cook for ten to fifteen minutes longer and then serve with fried bread or baked crusts.

Vegetable Mulligatawny (Thick)

Ingredients.—2lb. mixed vegetables, including celery (or use celery seed tied in a muslin bag), three pints of peelings stock or water, one dessertspoonful curry powder, one tablespoonful flour, a small piece of fat, half a gill of milk, and boiled rice. *Method.*—Cut the vegetables into small pieces, and put all in a pan with the water or stock. Bring to the boil, and then simmer gently until the vegetables are reduced to pulp. Pass through a sieve, mix a dessertspoonful of curry powder smoothly with the tablespoonful of flour, the fat and milk, and cook for fifteen minutes. Stir into the soup. Bring to the boil, and serve with boiled rice.

Tomato Soup

Ingredients.—¾lb. tomatoes, one pint vegetable stock, one bay leaf, a sprig of parsley, a stick of celery or a little celery seed tied in a bag, six peppercorns, a teaspoonful of sugar, one onion, a little fat, one tablespoonful of cornflour, salt to taste. Cornflour is better to use than flour with tomatoes as it does not alter the colour of the tomatoes as much as flour. *Method.*—Put the tomatoes and shredded onion into a pan with the stock, bay leaf, parsley, celery, peppercorns, and sugar, and simmer gently until the tomatoes are soft. Meanwhile fry the onion (sliced) in fat, and be careful that it does not brown. Then add to it the cornflour, mixed smooth with a little cold milk or stock, and add to the tomato, mix well, and let it boil, stirring till it thickens; simmer ten minutes. Add salt to taste. Pass through a fine sieve, and heat again. Serve with a tiny slice of fried bread.

Cream of Barley Soup

Ingredients.—One quart of stock, 2oz. finely ground barley, one pint and a gill of milk, the yolk of one egg. *Method.*—Mix the barley smoothly with the gill of milk and add it to the quart of boiling stock, and continue to boil it quickly for ten minutes. Mix the raw yolk of egg with the milk. Add this mixture by degrees to the soup, which must be boiling. Strain it into the tureen, and serve with fried croûtons.

Brown Haricot Soup

Ingredients.—1lb. of brown haricot beans (previously soaked overnight), two large carrots, one small turnip, the roots and outer parts of two heads of celery, two large onions, three quarts of water, two sprigs of parsley, one tablespoonful of red-currant jelly or the juice of half a lemon, quarter of a teaspoonful of mace, two teaspoonfuls of mixed herbs, 1oz. of fat, pepper and salt to taste. *Method.*—Soak the beans overnight and stew in a casserole for five or six hours. Pour off some of the stock or water. Peel and slice the onions, and fry in the fat until slightly browned; add the other vegetables and the stock, and cook till tender. Put in the herbs and spice for the last half-hour. Rub all through a wire sieve, using as many of the beans as will make it of the right consistency. Add the jelly or the lemon-juice, and a teaspoonful of sherry, and serve very hot with forcemeat balls in it.

Celery Soup

Ingredients.—One head of white celery, two large onions, one blade of mace, one bay leaf, 2oz. of rice, twelve peppercorns, one teaspoonful of sweet herbs tied in a muslin bag, 1oz. of fat, 1oz. of flour, quarter pint of milk, pepper and salt. *Method.*—Melt the fat in a large saucepan. Slice the onions, wash the celery (cut into small pieces), and fry both in the fat, without letting them brown. Add the rice and three pints of boiling white stock, and stew till tender. Put in the peppercorns and seasoning, and simmer ten minutes longer. Remove the peppercorns and herbs, and then rub through a sieve. Return to the saucepan, reheat, and add the milk gradually just before serving.

White Haricot Soup

Ingredients.—1lb. haricots, two quarts water or haricot stock, one onion, one gill milk (or part milk and water), 2oz. fat. *Method.*—Soak the haricots overnight, melt the fat in a saucepan, strain the haricots and toss in the fat, add the water or white stock, bring to the boil, and simmer till the haricots are soft. Rub through a sieve, return to the saucepan, together with the liquor they were cooked in, bring to the boil, stirring all the time, add the milk, reheat, and serve.

Artichoke Soup

Ingredients. — 2lb. Jerusalem artichokes, three pints of any white stock, one gill milk and water, salt, pepper. *Method.*—Wash and peel the artichokes, put into a pan with the stock, bring to the boil, skim, and simmer till soft. Rub through a sieve, return to the saucepan, add the milk, and bring to the boil, stirring all the time. Season and serve. If rice or macaroni stocks are too thick a little water can be added to them before using.

Turnip Soup

Ingredients.—Twelve large turnips, 5oz. fat, two quarts any white vegetable stock as above, one gill of milk, little grated nutmeg. *Method.*—Peel and slice the turnips, melt the fat in a saucepan, add the turnips, and toss for five minutes. Make the stock hot and simmer till the turnips are tender. Rub through a fine sieve, return to the saucepan, bring to the boil, skim, add the milk, season, reheat, and serve.

III
SAUCES, WITH AND WITH-OUT FAT

SPECIAL NOTE

When no fat can be spared sauces may be made without it as described, but they are of course not so nourishing.

G.R. Flour, i.e. Government Regulation or War Flour as now used.

III
SAUCES, WITH AND WITH-OUT FAT

NEEDED IN MANY OF THE FOLLOWING RECIPES

SAUCES WITHOUT FAT

White Sauce ($\frac{1}{2}$ a pint)

Ingredients.—$\frac{1}{2}$oz. of G.R. flour or 1oz. of cornflour, a gill of milk, a gill of water, or a gill of cereal stock (water in which rice, macaroni, or beans have been cooked), half a peeled onion with two cloves stuck into it, salt and pepper. *Method.*—Put all but two tablespoonfuls of the half-pint of liquid into a pan with the onion and cloves and bring it to the boil. Meanwhile put the flour into a basin and mix into it by degrees the cold liquid. Stir until the mixture becomes quite smooth. Strain on to it slowly the boiling liquid and stir thoroughly.

59

Return to the pan, bring to the boil again, season, and then simmer gently for five minutes. Serve plain or add chopped parsley, capers, anchovy essence, or chopped hard-boiled egg, or stir in 1oz. to 2oz. of finely grated dry cheese or two onions cooked, chopped, and sieved.

If a more nourishing sauce is needed add an egg, fresh or dried (if dried, soak according to directions given on the box), add to the cold flour and liquid mixture, and beat up well; then continue as before.

Cheese cannot always be procured and is often very new. Try to hoard a small piece until it dries, and use this for grating. Eggs and cheese contain fat as well as protein, and therefore add to the nourishment. Milk also contains fat, so that, strictly speaking, these sauces are not fatless, though they do not contain mixtures which we are accustomed to term fat, such as margarine or dripping.

A Sweet Sauce

This sauce, without pepper, salt, or onion, is made in the same fashion as the savoury white sauce, using cornflour and milk and water. It is then sweetened with sugar (one teaspoonful suffices), honey, jam, or ginger syrup.

Brown Sauce ($\frac{1}{2}$ a pint)

Ingredients.—Half an ounce of G.R. flour, half a pint of brown stock, a little Oxo, marmite, etc. *Method.*—Proceed as before, and at the last add a very little Bovril, Oxo, marmite or browning to improve the colour.

To vary the sauce add a spoonful or two of tomato purée, onion purée (minced, fried until soft and brown, and sieved), a few drops of ketchup, or a little sieved chutney.

Sauce for Binding Rissoles

may be made in the same way, but needs to be thicker; therefore use 2oz. of flour to half a pint of liquid.

Needless to say, these sauces are war sauces —makeshifts, but wholesome and palatable makeshifts—and, if carefully prepared and seasoned, superior to the lumpy, bill-sticker's paste-like concoction so often served under the name of sauce.

SAUCES WITH A LITTLE FAT

When stock is mentioned, vegetable or " peelings " stock or bone stock, or for white sauces the rice or macaroni stock, for which recipes have been given, should be used.

The thickening of almost all sauces is made of flour and butter (or in these days fat of any kind, including nut or cocoa butter). This mixture is called *Roux*, and can be white or brown.

English cooks generally seem to like to make this thickening (used also for soups) every time they require it. It would save time and material to make a week's supply and keep it in clean, well-corked, wide-necked jars. To make

Roux (White)

take 1oz. of fat and melt it. Then stir in 2oz. of flour and stir over a mild fire until you have a smooth paste. If you wish a richer thickening use equal quantities of flour and fat.

For half a pint of sauce about 1oz. of each or 1oz. of fat to 1½oz. flour or 1oz. fat to 2oz.

of flour would be needed. For a week's supply
use about ½lb. of fat and ¾lb. to 1lb. of flour.

Brown Roux

Proceed as before, but cook gently until the
paste browns lightly.

A useful well-flavoured

Brown Sauce

Ingredients.—1 onion, half a turnip, half a
carrot, 1oz. celery, teaspoonful of chopped
parsley, 8 peppercorns, 2 cloves, salt, 1
tomato, ¾ pint of stock (dark), 1oz. of glaze,
1½oz. of brown roux, 1oz. of fat. *Method.*
—Melt the fat, slice the vegetables, and
brown in the fat. Add the celery, parsley,
seasoning. Add 1 gill (quarter of a pint) of
stock and cook gently until the mixture is a
reddish brown. Now add half a pint of
stock, bring to the boil and then simmer for
three-quarters of an hour. Strain, taste,
and add salt and pepper as needed. Then
add the brown roux and simmer and stir
until smooth, and lastly stir in the glaze.
This sauce may be flavoured to taste, using
more tomato or none, a little sherry, a

spoonful of chutney or pickle, and I have known it served with a garnish of sultana raisins which have been plumped out in boiling water. It is, when properly made, a smooth, rich, dark brown sauce.

Melted Butter (White Sauce, Hot)

Ingredients.—1oz. of fat, 2oz. of flour, half a pint of milk, vegetable or cereal stock, or water, a few drops of lemon juice, white pepper, and salt. *Method.*—Melt the fat in a pan, and sprinkle in the flour (the less flour you put the richer the sauce will be), stir until the sauce will leave a clean place in the pan when lifted up in the spoon. Pour in very gradually the milk, stock, or water, stirring all the time to prevent any lumps. If any are seen, beat the sauce to a smooth paste before adding the rest of the liquid. When this is done, boil for ten to twelve minutes, stirring occasionally. Strain, season with a few drops of lemon juice and some white pepper and salt.

A richer sauce is made by adding one or two eggs well stirred in at the last, but the sauce must not boil after egg is added.

Dried eggs soaked according to directions on box may be used if necessary.

Egg Sauce (Hot)

Ingredients.—One egg, half a pint of melted butter sauce, a little lemon juice or vinegar, white pepper. *Method.*—Boil the egg for twelve minutes, and put it in cold water until it is hard, chop it finely, and add to the sauce. Heat it, and season with the lemon juice or vinegar and white pepper and salt if required.

Celery Sauce (Hot)

Ingredients.—Three or four small celery heads, some stock, 2oz. white roux, one cupful of milk, a blade of mace, and salt. *Method.*—Wash the celery and cut it into small pieces and boil in salt water for twenty minutes. Then drain and put into a clean saucepan, covering them with stock. Add salt and mace and stew all until tender. Take the roux, melt it and stir in the milk. When quite smooth mix with the celery and stock. Make thoroughly hot for about fifteen

E

minutes, but do not let it boil. Then sieve the sauce and reheat it.

The roots and outer leaves of the celery may be used and the inner part kept to serve as a vegetable.

Onion Sauce (Hot)

Ingredients.—Two large onions, 1oz. of fat, half a pint of melted butter sauce, made with milk or half milk and half rice or macaroni stock. *Method.*—Peel the onions and put them in boiling water for five minutes to blanch them, strain, and cut the onions into small pieces. Put them in a pan with the clarified fat, stew until tender. Lift the pan from the fire and stir in the melted butter. Let it boil, skim carefully, stir over the fire till it reduces a little, and rub through a hair sieve.

Bread Sauce

A mock bread sauce may be made with maize semolina

Ingredients.—One gill breadcrumbs, half a pint of milk, one small onion, two cloves, salt, pepper. *Method.*—Put the milk on to boil, with the onion peeled, in which have been stuck two cloves. When the milk is boiling add the breadcrumbs and stand the pan over very gentle heat till the bread has absorbed the milk and become thick. Take out the onion and cloves, add the seasoning, reheat and serve. If too thick add a little more milk.

Chutney Sauce (Hot)

Ingredients.—Four tablespoonfuls of chutney, six tablespoonfuls of brown roux melted, a little French mustard, one tablespoonful of ketchup, one tablespoonful of vegetable stock. *Method.*—Boil all together for three minutes, rub through a sieve and serve.

Curry Sauce (Hot)

Ingredients.—One onion, 1oz. fat, half dessertspoonful curry powder, one dessertspoonful flour, quarter of a pint stock, half an apple, salt to taste. *Method.*—Slice the onion in thin rings and fry in the clarified fat until quite soft. Stir in the curry powder and flour and fry a few minutes, adding salt to taste.   Add the stock and apple and cook all together for thirty minutes.   Add a teaspoonful of chutney if you have it.   Put the sauce through a sieve, make very hot, and use.   If too thick add a little more stock.

Tomato Sauce (Hot)

Ingredients.—Six small tomatoes, 1oz. roux, parsley, salt, pepper, a pinch of cayenne, one teaspoonful of anchovy essence, one pint of vegetable stock.   *Method.*—Cut the tomatoes into slices and place them in an enamelled saucepan, some chopped parsley, salt, pepper, and cayenne.   Pour over the vegetable stock. Boil until quite soft, sieve ; add the anchovy essence and the roux.   Stir over the fire, sieve, and serve very hot.   Tinned tomatoes may be used, and should be drained dry of the liquor in which they are preserved. The liquor should be used to flavour soup.

IV
SOME SEMI-MEATLESS DISHES

IV

SOME SEMI-MEATLESS DISHES

EXCELLENT AND ECONOMICAL

A Meat and Vegetable Pudding

Ingredients.—Half a pound of unsalted silver-side, shin, or stewing steak, two large Spanish onions, 2oz. of washed rice, two potatoes, stock (vegetable or bone stock), seasoning, suet pastry. *Method.*—Take a quart basin and grease it. Line it with pastry. Now cut the meat into strips, season with pepper and roll, wrapping a little piece of fat in each roll. Flour the rolls. Peel the onions and cut them up into eight pieces each, slice the potatoes, and arrange all the ingredients in layers. Add salt. Moisten each layer with stock, place the paste over the pudding, cover with greased paper, and steam for four and a half hours quite evenly and gently. Serve with a clean napkin pinned round the basin. Enough for six persons.

Suet Pastry

Ingredients.—3oz. suet or any fat, salt, one teaspoonful of baking-powder, 1lb. of flour. *Method.*—Chop very finely, 3oz. of shredded suet or any fat procurable. Dredge it with flour. Add one teaspoonful of salt and one of baking-powder to what is left after the dredging of 1lb. of dry sifted flour. Mix in the suet and then mix to a smooth, pliant, but not a wet, paste, with cold water. Line the greased basin with the paste and press the top round of paste well over the edge of the basin.

An Economical Pie

Ingredients.—Half a pound of beef (as for meat pudding), one hard-boiled egg sliced, one rasher of bacon cut into dice, ½lb. of cooked macaroni cut into short lengths, stock, seasoning, pastry. *Method.*—Cut the meat into pieces and add a very little fat cut small, flour, pepper and salt the meat and place the ingredients all mixed together in the dish. Pour in plenty of well-flavoured stock and cover with pastry. Wet the edge of the pie-dish before putting on a strip of paste round it and fit well down. Now put the pastry over, having wetted the first rim of pastry so that the two layers of paste will stick together. Dent with the prongs of a fork to make a neat edge and trim close to the edge of the pie-dish with a knife. Have some leaves of pastry ready to ornament the pie (these are cut out with fancy tin-cutters), and make a hole in the centre of the crust and have an ornament baked separately ready to put over it. Bake in a quick oven for fifteen minutes and then in a cool place (lower shelf of oven) for one and a quarter hour. Cover the crust with greased paper during this time, so that it shall not burn while the meat is cooking thoroughly. Ten minutes before serving, take out and add more stock, well-flavoured, through the hole in the pastry. Put on the ornament, and replace in the oven to become thoroughly hot. Egg for glazing should not be allowed.

A Plain Pie Pastry

Ingredients.—2oz. of fat, salt, ¾lb. of flour, water, and 1 teaspoonful of baking-powder. *Method.*—Mix salt, baking-powder, and flour. Rub in the fat with clean finger-tips until the mixture looks rather like coarse bread-crumbs. Mix to a rather dry paste with cold water. Roll firmly and lightly and use directly the paste is made.

Mince Fritters

Take any pieces of meat (several kinds for choice) and cut into tiny squares and be sure they are free of skin and gristle, which should go into the stock-pot. Dust with salt and pepper and a little powdered herb. Stir this into some batter and fry a tablespoonful at a time. Drain and serve very hot. About a dessertspoonful of mince serves for each fritter.

An Economical Batter made without Eggs

Ingredients.—4oz. flour, a pinch of salt, a quarter of a pint (gill) of tepid water, one tablespoonful of salad oil. *Method.*—Sift the flour and the salt, mix the oil and tepid water, and add the flour, gradually beating very well. Let the batter stand at least one hour before using. If a sweet batter is needed, add sugar instead of salt. For frying see directions given later.

Savoury Cassolettes

To use up pieces, take a kidney, a rasher of bacon, slice of ham, a mushroom, any pieces of meat, almost anything of a savoury kind that you have, mince into squares, season well, and mix in a pan with well-flavoured brown sauce, adding boiled rice or cooked and sieved lentils if there is not enough meat.

Prepare rounds of bread, the circumference of a tumbler and three and a half inches deep, and carefully cut out the centre. Fry the case golden brown in boiling fat, drain, and fill with the mince and sauce, and serve very hot. The bread cases must be neat and the bread must be rather stale, or it will not cut neatly. Use sharp tin-cutters to cut the bread and be sure that every crumb left is put back in the bread-pan.

How to Fry

To fry you should have half a stewpanful of clarified fat and a wire frying-basket to fit. Bring the fat to the boil with the basket in it. Then place the articles to be fried in the basket and see that they are at once covered with the boiling fat, and cook until they turn a golden brown. Then remove, drain free of grease, and they are ready for use. The fat may be reclarified and used over and over again with a little more added as required. It is necessary when frying that the fat shall be hotter than boiling-point. When boiling it bubbles, but when sufficiently hot for frying it becomes still and a very faint blue smoke rises. The reason that it must be brought to this degree of heat is that otherwise it does not at once seal the outside of the article to be fried and so prevent grease from penetrating into it. Also, there must be enough fat to cover the article entirely for the same reason. Never fill the pan too full and watch carefully that the fat does not overheat. If fat becomes badly burned it is useless. Rissoles, fillets of fish, fritters, croûtons are all fried in this fashion, which is known as deep frying, and is practically boiling in liquid fat. If you are doubtful if the fat is sufficiently hot try it with a piece of stale bread. If it becomes crisp and golden brown quickly, the fat is ready. If it becomes hard and dark, the fat is too hot.

To Clarify Fat

Melt the fat by slow degrees and when liquid let it cool a little, and then pour it into a clean basin. Then pour boiling water on it and let it stand until it becomes hard. The fat will form a clean cake on the top of the water. Any sediment, etc., adhering to the underpart may be scraped away. All fat from meat and soup skimmings should be clarified and kept in a clean basin ready for use.

Why Fat becomes Brown

Some cooks complain that the fat from roasted meat (when roasted in a gas-oven) becomes brown and so cannot be used for pastry and cake-making. The reason of this is that the baking-pan is put in the wrong place. It should stand at the bottom of the stove *under* the gas-jets, not on a shelf over them, as then the fat is cooking all the time and becomes brown. The joint should be placed on one of the grid-shelves or hung from one.

Fats for Non-Meat-Eaters

Those people who are non-meat-eaters do not, of course, use meat fats, but employ nut butter, cocoa butter, or oil.

Croûtons and Canapés

are made in the same way as cassolettes, but are generally flat pieces of bread only about a third of an inch thick. Those used for savouries are as a rule about the size of a sherry glass.

Raised Roman Pie

Ingredients.—$\frac{1}{2}$ lb. flour, 2oz. of any kind of fat, one teaspoonful baking-powder, pinch of salt, water to mix, $\frac{1}{2}$lb. cooked meat (beef or mutton), 4oz. cooked macaroni, one onion, chopped parsley (about one teaspoonful), a teaspoonful of sweet herbs. Brown sauce (see Sauces), salt, pepper. *Method.*—Free the meat from fat and gristle and cut into dice. Shred the onion finely and cook in 1oz. of fat till tender, but not too brown. Strain off the fat and add the onion to the meat with the herbs and parsley. Cut the macaroni into short lengths and add. Warm some good brown sauce and stir all the ingredients into it, season.

For the pastry, sift the flour, salt, and baking-powder into a basin, rub in the fat with the tips of the fingers, make a well in the centre, and add some water, stir the flour in gradually and mix all into a fairly stiff dough. Flour a board, put the dough on to it, flour a rolling-pin and roll out about a quarter of an inch thick. Have a greased cake-tin ready, line it with pastry, keeping back enough to form a lid. Fill the centre with the meat mixture, roll out the pastry lid to the required size, brush over the edges with water, fit on the lid and press the edges well together. Ornament the edges with the back of a knife or a fork, make some leaves and an ornament for the centre with trimmings of pastry and put on. Bake in a hot oven from half to three-quarters of. an hour. When the pastry is quite cooked, turn the pie out of the tin very carefully, so as not to break it, and dish.

Cornish Pasties

Ingredients.—2oz. meat, uncooked, two potatoes, one onion, one tablespoonful of water, pepper and salt. For the paste, ½lb. flour, half teaspoonful of baking-powder, 1½oz. fat, water to mix. *Method.*—Cut the meat, onion, and potato into quite small dice and mix with the pepper, salt, and the water on a plate. If the vegetables were not cut small they would be undercooked by the time the pastry was finished. Rub the dripping into the flour, add a pinch of salt and the baking-powder, and mix to a firm paste with a little cold water. Roll it out on a board, cut out some rounds, place a portion of the meat and vegetables on each, wet the edges, and pinch together firmly, so that the join comes at the top. Mark edges with a fork to form a goffered border. Place on a floured baking-tin, and bake in a hot oven for fifteen minutes and then fifteen minutes in a lower heat. Cornish pasties proper are made with raw meat and vegetables, but cooked meat and vegetables mixed with a little sauce can be used.

Haricot Beans and Bacon en Casserole

Ingredients.—Half a pint haricot beans, two rashers of bacon, one small boiled onion, pepper and salt. *Method.*—Wash and soak the beans overnight in cold water. Put them and the water in which they were soaked in a casserole. When thoroughly hot, add more cold water and cook slowly for two to three hours. Shred the onion. Cut the bacon into strips, fry in a frying-pan, put in the onion, and stir over the fire for a few minutes. Add the onion and bacon to the beans, season with pepper, and cook slowly till tender, stirring occasionally to prevent burning. Add the salt only about twenty minutes before serving in the casserole in which they are cooked.

Hot-Pot of Mutton with Pearl Barley

Ingredients.—The best end of a neck of mutton, margarine or dripping, one Spanish onion, seasoning, parsley, mixed herbs, two kidneys, half a pint of stock, 4oz. pearl barley. *Method.*—Take the meat from the best end of a neck of mutton, remove as

F

much fat as possible, flour it and fry in a frying-pan in any hot fat just to brown the meat. Place it in an earthenware casserole, add one Spanish onion cut in eight, salt and pepper. Tie in muslin ten peppercorns, two cloves, a spray of parsley, a pinch of mixed spice and herbs. If possible add two sheep's kidneys with the cores removed and cut in quarters and 4oz. of pearl barley which has been simmered in stock or water for one hour. Add a pint of the stock, cover and cook quite gently for two hours. Strain off the gravy, thicken it and brown it; remove the muslin and its contents. With a spoon collect the meat in the centre of the casserole with the barley round and over, and pour the sauce over. Serve very hot.

Noisettes of Mutton and Pearl Barley

Pearl barley may be used with stewed noisettes or steak. It simply needs to be cooked in stock and well seasoned.

Mutton and Rice Stew

Ingredients.—2lb. scrag end of neck of mutton, 3lb. of onion, carrot, turnip, mixed seasoning, parsley, 2oz. rice. *Method.*—Take the scrag end of a neck of mutton and wash it. Then divide it and remove what fat you can. Place it in a pan with an onion, a carrot, and a turnip cut into dice, salt, pepper, and some shred parsley, also 2oz. of rice. Cover and simmer quite gently for four hours. Before serving remove the bones, leaving the meat in the broth. The proportions are about 2lb. of scrag to 3lb. of vegetables and two quarts of water. Taste the broth to see that it is well seasoned, and serve very hot.

Small Dumplings (for serving with the Barley Broth)

Ingredients.—½lb. of wholemeal flour, 1oz. of any clarified fat. *Method.*—Rub the fat into the flour, moisten with a little water, form into balls the size of a marble and drop into boiling water or stock and cook about thirty minutes, or they can be cooked in a saucepan with boiled beef, fresh or salt, and can be served round the dish with meat.

Stuffed Meats and Meat with Dumplings, Yorkshire Pudding, Savoury Cakes, etc.

These can scarcely come under the heading of semi-meatless dishes, though if enough stuffing, etc., is used they perhaps might do so.

Of this economical order of joint is shoulder of mutton, roasted or braised, stuffed with savoury rice, potato, or savoury stuffing.

Stuffed and rolled neck of mutton (for which a recipe is given).

Beefsteak stuffed, rolled, pot roasted or braised (this is economical because there is practically no waste with steak).

Beef olives. With a lavish supply of stuffing and gravy served with savoury rice, and made from steak or fresh silverside.

Fresh silverside is one of the cheapest joints as there is but little bone or fat. A piece of 7lb. provides :

Braised beef with vegetables and macaroni, $3\frac{1}{2}$lb. (excellent hot or cold).

Meat pie (see recipe) for six, $\frac{1}{2}$lb. meat.

Raised Roman pie (see recipe) for six, 1lb. meat.

Beef olives, for six, $1\frac{1}{4}$lb. meat.

War galantine (see recipe), for six, ½lb. meat.

Other substantial dishes needing but little meat are :

Jugged rabbit (with forcemeat balls and Spanish onion).

Irish stew (made with rice or pearl barley, potatoes, and onions).

Roman mince (see recipe).

Boiled salted silverside with dumplings and carrots, turnips and onions.

Roast meat with Yorkshire pudding or savoury cake (see recipe), and a dish or rice or pearl barley stewed in stock or macaroni.

With these suggestions to go upon the cook will soon be able to add to the list of economical meats.

SOME STUFFING FOR JOINTS

Potato Stuffing

Ingredients.—Two breakfastcupfuls of mashed potatoes (hot), one tablespoonful of chopped parsley, one teaspoonful of chopped onion, one teaspoonful (level) of powdered herbs, two tablespoonfuls of milk, one dried egg, one tablespoonful of warmed fat, salt.

and pepper. *Method.*—Beat the egg, melt the dripping and beat into the potato with the other ingredients, and use sufficient milk to bind it.

Savoury Stuffing

Proceed as above, but use half quantity of potato and make up with a purée of any cheap cooked vegetable (Spanish onion, leek, tomato, or carrot, for example), or rice boiled in stock, and flavoured with salt and pepper.

Sage and Onion Stuffing

Ingredients.—½lb. bread-crumbs, two Spanish onions, twelve sage leaves, salt, pepper. *Method.*—Peel the onion, put into cold water, bring to the boil and boil till getting a little soft. Strain and chop finely. Add to the bread-crumbs, chop the sage and add, season and mix with a tablespoonful of milk. It is then ready for use.

Sweet Herb Stuffing

Ingredients.—6oz. fine stale crumbs, 3oz. of chopped suet, two teaspoonfuls each of powdered thyme and marjoram, a large tablespoonful of chopped parsley, half a lemon rind, grated; one egg, salt, pepper. (Crust and crumb may be used, and the quickest way to reduce it to crumbs is to put it through the mincer.) *Method.*—Beat the egg well, and mix with all the other ingredients. If suet is not to hand, use any clarified fat, and if eggs are dear milk may be used for binding the stuffing.

Forcemeat Balls

Ingredients.—8oz. of stale bread, crust and crumb, stock, 1oz. of fat, two teaspoonfuls of minced onion, two teaspoonfuls minced parsley (use stalks too), pepper, salt, grated lemon rind, one egg. *Method.*—Soak the bread-crumbs in the stock and squeeze dry. Mix with the fat, onions, parsley, pepper, salt, and grated lemon rind. Well beat the egg, and mix well with the bread-crumbs, etc. Form into balls. Fry lightly and add to the stew a few minutes before serving.

Dumplings

Ingredients.—½lb. flour, 1½oz. of suet or finely shred fat, half teaspoonful of baking-powder, about three-quarters of a teacupful of water. *Method.*—Mix the flour, suet or fat, and baking-powder with the water. Flour the hands and roll the mixture into balls. Cook in the gravy of the stew for thirty minutes. The gravy should be boiling when the balls are added and there must be enough to cover them. If not, cook in boiling water and add before serving. If necessary omit all fat in this recipe.

Savoury Cake

Ingredients.—6oz. of bread-crumbs, a little stock, 2oz. of either minced suet or the superfluous fat from the joint cut off either before or after cooking, dripping or nut butter, one onion, quarter of a teaspoonful sieved sweet herbs, one egg, salt. *Method.*— Soak the bread-crumbs in the stock, and mix well with the minced suet, dripping, or nut butter, three tablespoonfuls of chopped onion, quarter of a teaspoonful of sieved sweet herbs, one egg, or a little milk, and salt to taste. After mixing all well together, fill a greased tin with the mixture, and bake in a moderate oven till golden brown on top.

Cut into portions, and serve with each portion of roast or grilled meat, or serve with vegetables and sauce or gravy instead of meat.

War Galantine

Ingredients.—4oz. of raw beef, 8oz. cooked red lentils, 4oz. sausage meat, 6oz. fine dry bread-crumbs, one teaspoonful each of chopped parsley, grated onion, and mixed herbs. Salt and pepper to taste. *Method.*—Mix all the ingredients with one dried egg beaten up with about one gill of stock. Form into a roll and tie in a well-floured clean cloth, leaving room for the roll to swell. The cloth must be wrung out in boiling water before flouring or the flour would not adhere. Place in boiling stock or water and simmer for two hours. Remove, tie up tighter and press. When cold glaze. If preferred add two ounces of chopped nuts to the galantine. The stock or water it was cooked in, if well skimmed, should be used as a foundation for a thick soup.

Roman Mince

Ingredients.—4oz. any kind of cold meat, ¾lb. cooked macaroni, 2oz. grated cheese, half pint of brown or tomato sauce. Brown bread-crumbs, salt, pepper, one teaspoonful chopped parsley. *Method.*—Mince the meat and mix with the sauce and parsley. Grease a pie-dish and put in a layer of cooked macaroni, then a layer of the meat and sauce. Sprinkle over half the cheese and continue putting in alternate layers of macaroni and meat, having the top layer macaroni. Sprinkle the other half of the cheese over the last layer, cover with brown bread-crumbs, if possible put little pieces of fat over the bread-crumbs, and bake in moderate oven about fifteen minutes.

Neck of Mutton, Rolled and Stuffed

Ingredients.—The best way of buying this is to get the whole neck of mutton or lamb, and keep the best end for cutlets or a roast and the extreme end of the scrag for mutton broth. Take the middle and best end of the scrag and remove all the bones and some of the superfluous fat, lay flat upon a table or board and press out well with a broad knife, then spread over a forcemeat made as follows: ½lb. bread-crumbs, one tablespoonful chopped parsley, half table-spoonful sweet herbs, 1oz. fat, grated rind of a lemon, salt and pepper, egg or milk to bind. *Method.*—Put the crumbs into a basin, add the fat chopped, the grated lemon rind, parsley, and herbs. Beat up the egg and mix all well together, add a little milk if necessary, or it can be mixed with milk instead of egg if liked. Spread this force-meat over the boned meat, roll it up and tie with string. Put it into a saucepan or casserole, pour in some brown sauce, about a pint, and simmer gently, one to two hours according to the size of the roll. Take out and put in a hot oven or under the grill to brown. Serve on a hot dish with the sauce poured round. If cooked in a casserole it can be sent to table in the casserole. Be sure to keep the lid on all the time it is cooking, and look at it from time to time to see it does not burn. It can be served with any vegetable. If liked it can be stuffed with a sage and onion stuffing, and be served with apple sauce.

When so small a quantity of meat may be bought it is better to use it fresh rather than to re-cook it and thereby lose nourishment.

V
PULSE DISHES

NOTE

Many of these dishes can be made without fat, but as pulses contain no natural fat some should be added whenever possible.

V
PULSE DISHES

PULSES (otherwise *legumens*) are peas and
beans and lentils. With the exception of red
(Egyptian) lentils, all dried pulses must be
soaked for quite twelve hours and cooked
long and slowly, and salt should not be added
until the last few minutes of cooking. The
fresh pulses—green peas, broad beans, etc.,
are dealt with in the chapter on vegetable
dishes. Pulses are rich in protein, but contain no fat. Fat, therefore, should always
be added when cooking.

Some people find pulses indigestible, but
this is often because they are insufficiently
soaked and cooked. They need long and slow
cooking. Often, too, they are found indigestible when eaten with meat, the combi-
nation of two foods containing such a high
proportion of protein throwing too great a

strain on the digestive organs. Again, persons unable to eat pulses cooked whole can often take them if put through a sieve.

The Skins of Beans

Some people find the skins of all kinds of beans, haricots, butter beans, brown haricots, etc., indigestible—in which case it is best to remove the skins after cooking the beans, before serving them, in those dishes where the beans are served whole, not rubbed through a sieve. Very often when well boiled the skins become loose and float in the water, when it is easy to skim them off, otherwise it is a tedious task to skin all the beans. Brown beans especially have very hard skins. For people who find the beans cause indigestion it is best to eat only the dishes where the pulse foods are rubbed through a sieve.

Lentil Roast (Red Lentils)

Ingredients.—½lb. lentils, ¼lb. mashed potatoes, ¼lb. bread-crumbs, two Spanish onions, chopped parsley, salt, pepper, 1oz. of fat. *Method.*—Wash the lentils, put into a saucepan with the fat and shredded onions, stir for five minutes, pour over one pint of vegetable or cereal stock or water, bring to the boil and cook very gently till soft. More stock can be added if necessary, but it must be fairly dry when the lentils are cooked. Drain off any superfluous stock, add the mashed potatoes, bread-crumbs, chopped parsley, and seasoning, mix well together, form into a shape as much like roast duck as possible, put into a well-greased dripping-tin, cover with small scraps of fat, and bake in a fairly hot oven, basting often, till a nice brown. It should be served on a hot dish with a good brown or tomato sauce poured round, and if liked red-currant jelly can be handed with it.

This can be made in the same manner with more onion and sage instead of parsley, and should then be eaten with brown sauce and apple sauce handed round.

Lentil Cutlets (Red Lentils)

Ingredients.—½lb. lentils, ¼lb. rice, one small onion, one carrot, 1oz. fat, one pint vegetable stock, salt, pepper. *Method.*—

G

Wash the rice and lentils, peel and slice the onion, scrape the carrot, and cut into dice. Melt the fat in a saucepan, add the lentils, rice, and vegetables, and stir for five minutes, add the stock, bring to the boil and simmer until the lentils, etc., are tender. Add more stock if necessary and be careful not to let it burn. When cooked it must be a fairly stiff mixture. Season and turn on to a plate to cool, then form it into cutlets on a floured board, coat the cutlets with flour, put into a frying-basket, and plunge into very hot fat; fry a delicate brown, turn them on to a piece of kitchen paper to drain and dish in a circle on a dish-paper. Garnish with fried parsley. If frying is impossible place on a greased tin and bake in a fairly hot oven.

Lentil Patties (Red Lentils)

Ingredients.—¼lb. lentils, one onion, 1oz. of any kind of fat, pepper, salt, one pint vegetable stock, trimmings of pastry. *Method.*—Wash the lentils, slice the onion, melt the fat in a saucepan, add lentils and onion, stir five minutes, add the stock, bring to the boil, and simmer till the lentils are tender. If necessary add more stock, but they should absorb the stock. Mash them a little, season. Line some patty-pans with pastry, put in some of the lentil mixture, cover with pastry, and bake in a quick oven.

Haricot Bean Fritters

Ingredients.—½lb. haricot beans, ¼lb. bread-crumbs, one teaspoonful mixed herbs, one teaspoonful chopped parsley, one egg, salt, pepper, one and a half pint of water or stock. *Method.*—Wash the beans and soak them overnight. Put them into a saucepan with one and a half pint of the water they were soaked in, or the same quantity of white vegetable or cereal stock. Bring to the boil and simmer gently till tender—about three hours. If they get too dry add more stock. When soft rub through a sieve, add the herbs and chopped parsley, and seasoning. Beat up the yolk of an egg and mix all well together. Form into balls or shape like a cork, brush over with the slightly beaten white of the egg, roll in bread-crumbs and fry in hot fat.

Haricot and Butter Beans

Ingredients.—1lb. haricots or butter beans, one quart of water or vegetable stock, one tablespoonful chopped parsley, 1oz. fat or nutter, salt, pepper. *Method.*—Wash the beans and soak overnight in one quart of water. Put them into a saucepan with the water they were soaked in or in one quart of vegetable stock, and salt, bring to the boil, simmer gently till tender (about three hours), strain, melt the fat in a pan, add the beans and seasoning and make very hot—do not let them burn. Turn into a hot vegetable dish, sprinkle chopped parsley over, and serve.

Haricots and Tomatoes

Ingredients.—1lb. haricots or butter beans, half a pint of tomato sauce or purée of tomato, chopped parsley, salt, pepper, 1oz. of any kind of fat. *Method.*—Wash the beans, soak overnight in one quart of water. Put the fat into a saucepan, strain the beans and add, toss for two or three minutes, then add salt, the water they were soaked in, or vegetable stock, bring to the boil and simmer

till tender, strain. Put some thick tomato
sauce or purée into a pan and make it hot,
add the beans and seasoning, make them hot
and serve on squares of toast with chopped
parsley sprinkled over.

Haricot Mould

Ingredients.—1lb. haricots, one small onion,
one egg, ½lb. bread-crumbs, salt, pepper, 1oz.
of fat. *Method.*—Wash the haricots and
soak overnight, boil in the water they were
soaked in or in vegetable stock till tender.
Strain off the water and rub through a sieve,
add the bread-crumbs, chop the onion finely,
and fry till soft in the fat, add the beans and
bread-crumbs and beaten yolk of the egg
and mix well, cook till it forms a ball in the
middle of the pan, stirring all the time.
Turn on to a plate. Grease very well a
soufflé mould or cake-tin and coat with
brown or red bread-crumbs and line with
the haricot mixture. It should be at least
an inch thick both at the bottom and sides.
Slightly whip the white of egg and brush the
inside of the mixture and the top with it
bake in a fairly hot oven, till firm, from three-

quarters to one hour. Turn out without breaking and fill with tomato, rice, or macaroni, or cold cooked vegetables heated in brown or tomato sauce.

Casserole of Carrots, Butter Beans, and Onions

Ingredients.—1lb. butter beans, one onion, three carrots, a little salt, 1oz. of any kind of fat. *Method.*—Soak the beans overnight, and then place in cold water and boil them with the fat until soft. Chop the onion and fry it thoroughly; boil the carrots, slice them, and place them and the butter beans with the onion in the frying-pan, and stir about until quite hot. Add salt and pepper to taste. Serve very hot in a casserole.

Curried Butter Beans

Ingredients.—½lb. butter beans, one and a half pint of water, 1oz. of any fat available, curry sauce, salt. *Method.*—Wash the beans and soak overnight. Melt the fat in a saucepan, add the beans, stir for five minutes. Add one and a half pint of the water they were boiled in, some salt, and bring to the

boil, simmer till tender, strain. Put the
curry sauce (see Sauces) into a pan and make
hot, add the beans, and cook till quite hot,
then serve in a hot dish with a border of
boiled rice (see To Boil Rice, page 117)
round. Chutney can be handed round with
this.

Curried Yellow Lentils or Split Peas

Ingredients.—½lb. lentils or peas, one onion
chopped, 1oz. of any fat, one pint vegetable
stock, one teaspoonful curry powder, one
apple chopped, salt, pepper. *Method.*—Wash
and soak the lentils or peas overnight. Put
them into a pan with the stock, chopped
onion, and apple and salt, and cook gently
till soft. Add the fat and the curry powder,
salt and pepper, and cook another ten
minutes. If too dry, add a little coco-nut
milk made as follows : put two tablespoonfuls
of desiccated coco-nut into a basin, and pour
one gill of boiling water on to it. Let it
stand fifteen minutes, strain, and it is ready
for use. Dish the lentils in a hot vegetable
dish, and hand boiled rice in another with
them. A little chutney and grated coco-nut
are a great improvement handed with them.

Pease-Pudding

Ingredients.—One pint split peas, a bunch of herbs, 1oz. of fat, vegetable stock, gill of milk, pepper, salt. *Method.*—Grease a casserole all over and place in it the peas which have been soaked for twelve hours, pepper, a bunch of herbs, 1oz. of fat, and enough vegetable stock to cover the peas. Bring to the boil by slow degrees, cover and cook for three hours, skim once or twice, shake the pan now and then, and add more stock. When soft, remove the herbs, add salt to taste, and rub through a fine sieve. Replace in the pan, add the milk, mix thoroughly and when very hot serve in the casserole with snippets of fried bread or *fleurons* of pastry placed on the top.

Florentine Rissoles

Ingredients.—Pease-pudding, onion sauce, egg, crumbs. *Method.*—The pease-pudding mixture makes delicious rissoles. Let it cool, then form into shape, make a hole in each with a teaspoon handle and fill with onion sauce (page 66), made rather thick, close up, egg, crumb, and fry.

Faraday Croûtons

Ingredients.—Pease-pudding, tomatoes.
Method.—Use the pease-pudding to make small, round croûtons, flour, fry or bake. Serve a slice of grilled tomato on each and be sure they are very hot.

Savoury Oatmeal Pudding

Ingredients.—5oz. flour, 4oz. medium oatmeal, 1½oz. suet or of any other fat, one tablespoonful chopped parsley, one dessertspoonful mixed herbs, salt, pepper, stock, or vegetable stock or gravy to moisten it with, about one gill, one tablespoonful bakingpowder. *Method.*—Mix the flour, oatmeal, suet, parsley, herbs, and seasoning in a basin, moisten with the stock and mix well, put into a well-greased basin, covered with a floured-scalded cloth, and boil two hours, or better still, cover with a greased paper and steam three hours. It can be eaten cut in slices and put round a stew or hash, or can be eaten without meat served with a good brown sauce.

Dried Green Peas

Ingredients.—½lb. dried green peas, sprig of mint (either fresh or dried), 1oz. of fat if possible, salt, pepper, water. *Method.*—Wash the peas and soak them overnight. Put them into a saucepan with the water they were soaked in, the mint, salt, and a small piece of soda; bring to the boil and simmer till tender. Skim off any pieces or skin that rise while boiling, strain, melt the fat in a pan, add the peas and seasoning, and serve hot.

They can be added to meat in a meat pie after boiling in the above manner, or can be used in stews, or soups, or when cold, in salads. A nice purée can be made of them by cooking as above, then rubbing them through a sieve, returning to the saucepan with some of the water they were cooked in, and half a pint of milk. Bring to the boil, season and serve with fried bread. Some chopped or powdered mint should be put into the tureen and the soup poured over it. They also make a nice centre for a dish of cutlets, cooked as above.

Potted Beans

Ingredients.—¼lb. dried haricot beans, 1oz. grated cheese, 1oz. of any kind of fat, 1oz. bread-crumbs, ½oz. chopped onion, seasoning to taste. *Method.*—Soak the beans the previous day, then cook slowly till quite tender. Beat them through a sieve with the onion. Add the other ingredients. Stir vigorously over the fire for a few moments, then pound in a mortar or basin till perfectly smooth. Pot tightly and pour melted fat over the top. As an emergency food potted haricots are invaluable, and will keep ten days if stood in a cool place.

VI
CEREAL DISHES

.

VI
CEREAL DISHES

CEREALS are wheat, barley, maize (otherwise Indian corn or mealies), oats, rice, and, in addition, sago and tapioca (the former being the pith of the sago palm, the latter the root of the tapioca plant). Those persons who cannot digest pulse foods often find that cereals suit them admirably.

Macaroni (Home-made)

It is only in England that the admirable qualities of home-made macaroni appear to be almost unknown. The cooks of France add *nouilles* to soup or stew ; German housewives grudge neither time nor trouble spent in the preparation of the *nudeln* which afford so many attractive little dishes in themselves, as well as adding bulk and variety to other dishes ; but few Englishwomen appear to know how easily this class of Italian paste can be made at home.

111

Italian Paste

Ingredients.—½lb. of household flour, half a teaspoonful of salt, one egg, and two to three tablespoonfuls of cold water. *Method.*—Mix the flour and salt in a small basin and stir in the egg and water with knife. After a preliminary kneading in the basin the paste is rolled on a table or marble slab under the palms of both hands until it resembles a long roll, then reversed and gradually kneaded into a short roll with the palm of the right hand just above the wrist, applying considerable pressure. The alternate movements are continued from twenty to thirty minutes, until the paste is elastic and quite smooth. The paste is more easily handled if halved and rolled into two sheets almost as thin as paper instead of one larger one. Just a little flour may be sprinkled on the table, but none on the rolling-pin. Leave the sheets of paste spread out for about two hours. In this state the paste breaks easily, but cutting is speedily accomplished by means of a knife strong and sharp enough to go through many strips of paste placed one on top of the other. Though the paste may be cooked as soon as it is cut, it is better if kept overnight spread in single layers to harden before being used.

Nouilles or *nudeln* are made in just the same way, but as a rule a little batter and one or two more eggs are added. These, however, are not really necessary.

A still cheaper form of macaroni is made of

Water Paste

Ingredients.—½lb. flour, salt, boiling water. *Method.*—To half a pound of flour add a small level teaspoonful of salt, and after warming the flour, boiling water is stirred in gradually until half the flour is moistened, leaving the remainder to be kneaded in. Knead and cut as in the previous recipes.

Nouilles au Gratin

Ingredients.—3oz. nouilles, salt, boiling water, 1oz. of fat, half a pint of hot milk, one tablespoonful of grated cheese, bread-crumbs. *Method.*—Boil 3oz. of nouilles in salted water for fifteen minutes and drain. Melt one ounce of fat and stir in as much flour as it will moisten. When it has cooked gently for five minutes add a half-pint of hot milk, salt, pepper, and a grain or two of cayenne. Stir and boil gently till smooth, then withdraw from the fire and add a table-spoonful of grated cheese. Place the nouilles in a greased pie-dish in layers with the sauce spread between. Cover the final layer of nouilles lightly with mixed bread-crumbs and cheese, and bake in a fairly hot oven till nicely browned.

Ravioli Maigre

Ingredients.—½lb. Italian paste, 1lb. spinach one tablespoonful of chopped onion, fat, one tablespoonful of grated cheese. *Method.*— Prepare half a pound of Italian paste, roll it out as thin as possible, and dry it for one hour. Boil one pound of spinach in a little water, and after draining thoroughly chop it finely. In a little hot fat lightly brown a teaspoonful of very finely chopped onion, sprinkle in a heaped teaspoonful of flour, and when it has cooked for a few minutes stir in the spinach. Season to taste, and when cool stir in a small tablespoonful of cheese and put all through a sieve. Cut the paste into rounds one and a half inch in diameter; wet the edges of one half with water, place in the centre a little of the spinach, and cover with the remaining rounds of paste. Seal the edges by pressing them together, and drop the raviolis into boiling salted water. Boil them gently for about half an hour and drain them well. Serve in a fireproof dish with a little white sauce mixed with cheese, or with tomato sauce poured over.

This home-made macaroni is delicious just tossed in fat, seasoned with pepper and salt, and served with poached eggs or as a centre to cutlets or fillets, or with boiled chicken or rabbit, or for that matter plain, and it is infinitely superior to the hard, tasteless, stale macaroni so often bought in England.

To Boil Bought Macaroni

Do not wash, and omit the lemon juice. Otherwise treat exactly as for rice. Test with a fork to see when soft.

Macaroni and Celery

Ingredients.—Three heads of celery, one pint of milk and white vegetable stock, bay-leaf, 2oz. macaroni, half a pint white sauce, pepper, salt. *Method.*—Wash the celery, cut away the green leaves and any spoil outside pieces, which can be kept for stock. Put it into a saucepan with the milk and stock. Add the bay-leaf and boil till tender, drain and cut into short pieces, boil the macaroni in salted water, drain and cut into pieces about the same size as the celery. Warm the sauce, add the celery and macaroni, season, bring to the boil and simmer about ten minutes. Serve hot. A little cream added at the end improves this.

Macaroni and Tomatoes

Ingredients.—4oz. macaroni, half a pint of white sauce or melted butter, 1oz. of cheese, two tablespoonfuls of tomato sauce or half a pint of tomato purée, salt, pepper. *Method.* —Boil the macaroni until tender, drain, and mix with the white sauce, add half the cheese and seasoning and the tomato purée or sauce. Put into a greased fireproof dish, sprinkle the rest of the cheese over, and bake until brown, or put under a griller. Serve very hot. Spaghetti and rice can be used in the same way.

Macaroni and Potatoes (a Left-over Dish)

Ingredients.—Boiled macaroni, boiled potatoes, sauce, seasoning. *Method.*—Take any cooked macaroni or nouilles and some cooked sliced potato, mix with white sauce (egg, celery, soubise or bread sauce will serve or these may be mixed with some plain white sauce), grease a china soufflé dish. Fill with the mixture, cover with fine bread-crumbs and brown in a moderate oven.

Savoury Macaroni

Ingredients.—6oz. cooked macaroni (freshly made for choice), six tomatoes, seasoning, 6oz. risotto. *Method.*—Grease a china soufflé dish and fill it with layers of tomato purée (tomatoes stewed and sieved), risotto, and macaroni and plenty of seasoning. Finish with tomato and scatter with fine bread-crumbs. Place in the oven to brown and heat thoroughly.

To Boil Rice

Take a four-quart pan three-parts full of water. Bring it to boiling-point, with a dessertspoonful of salt and the juice of half a lemon. Wash the rice and dry it, place four ounces of it in the boiling water. Put a jug of cold water handy. Stir the rice now and then. In ten minutes test the rice by pinching a few grains between finger and thumb. When soft, add cold water to stop the boiling at once, drain, return the dry rice to a dry, hot pan. Shake well, cover with a napkin, set on a cool part of the stove and shake occasionally. Serve hot and dry. Each grain should be well swollen and separate from the other. For curry, use Patna rice—for other purposes Carolina.

Risotto (I)

Ingredients.—Half a pint of milk and water, small teacupful of raw rice, three onions, six good-sized tomatoes, 1oz. finely grated cheese, pepper and salt to taste. *Method.*—Place onions, tomatoes (both these ingredients should be chopped finely), pepper and salt into a saucepan with the milk, boil all together until soft, stirring occasionally, and adding more milk or water if necessary, sieve, then add the rice and cook until soft. Just before serving stir in the finely grated cheese.

Risotto (II)

Ingredients.—¼lb. of rice, one onion, one quart of stock, seasoning. *Method.*—Wash the rice, place it in the boiling stock, cook slowly with the lid on until the stock is absorbed—about one and a half hours. Watch that it does not burn. Slice, chop, and fry (without browning it) the onion, which will take about ten minutes if chopped very fine, add it to the rice with salt and pepper and serve very hot. This rice is quite good without any onion if made with well-flavoured stock.

Tomato Rice

Ingredients.—2oz. of rice, half a pint of stock, 1lb. of tomato purée, pepper and salt. *Method.*—Thoroughly wash the rice and cook in the stock until quite soft, then flavour with the pepper and salt. Take the tomato purée, add the rice and beat together until smooth. Serve very hot, with or without grated cheese, or as a border to a dish of stewed kidneys or boiled chicken.

Savoury Rice Soufflé

Ingredients.—2oz. of rice, stock, two or three teaspoonfuls of onion or tomato purée, three eggs. *Method.*—Cook the rice in the stock and season well, drain and let it cool, then stir in the onion or tomato purée, add the yolks of two eggs one at a time, then a whole egg, and then the frothed whites of two eggs. Bake in a greased soufflé-dish half full for ten minutes in a hot oven. If eggs are dear, omit the whole egg for this soufflé and use one dried egg.

Pilaff of Rice

Ingredients.—As for Risotto (No. II), 2oz. of nuts, 2oz. of sultana raisins. *Method.*—Make the risotto as before, fry separately the nuts, shred lengthwise, clean and fry quite lightly the sultanas, drain, and add to the onion-flavoured rice and serve very hot.

Fried Rice Cakes

Ingredients.—¼lb. rice, 1 oz. grated cheese, ½oz. finely chopped onion, ½oz. finely chopped parsley, 1oz. of fat, milk or stock. *Method.*

—Boil the rice and the onion, with a pinch of salt, until the rice is tender, and drain. Melt the fat in a saucepan, stir in the rice, the onion chopped finely, the cheese and parsley. Mix with a little stock or milk. Stir on the fire for a few minutes, then add one egg. Turn out on to dish to get cold, when the rice can be cut out in rounds, rolled in crumbs and fried or baked. Rice cakes may be served with vegetable, with buttered eggs, or they are a very good breakfast dish added to a small portion of fried bacon.

Savoury Ground Rice Soufflé (Hot)

Ingredients.—A little over a pint of milk, one tablespoonful of ground rice, 2oz. of finely grated cheese, two eggs, one dried, one fresh. *Method.*—Heat the milk and pour it on to the ground rice previously mixed with a little cold milk, return to the pan and stir until the mixture thickens. Remove the pan from the fire and add the grated cheese, a pinch of salt and cayenne, one dried egg and the yolk of one fresh egg. Mix all well together, and then add the beaten white of the egg. Grease a soufflé-dish and pour the mixture into it, and bake in a moderate oven for twenty minutes. Sprinkle grated cheese over the top before serving.

Semolina Pastry

Ingredients.—One pint of milk, a little salt, 5oz. of semolina, white pepper, 1½oz. grated cheese. *Method.*—Boil the milk. When boiling, drop in by degrees the semolina, stir until it thickens like a custard, which takes about fifteen minutes, add the pepper, salt, and grated cheese, spread on a floured board, and let it cool. It is then ready for use.

Semolina Cakes (Hot)

Ingredients.—One pint of milk, 4oz. of semolina, one egg, bread-crumbs (or batter), salt, white pepper. *Method.*—Boil the milk and a little salt. When boiling, drop into it by degrees the semolina and stir until it thickens like custard, which takes about fifteen minutes, add a little white pepper, spread the mixture out on a floured board—when cold it becomes sufficiently solid to form into cakes. Egg and crumb the cakes and fry a golden brown or bake, or dip in batter and fry or bake.

Gnocci (Hot)

Ingredients.—4oz. of semolina, 1oz. of grated cheese, one pint of water, salt. *Method.*—Boil the water with some salt. Drop in the semolina by degrees and stir until the mixture thickens (this will take about a quarter of an hour), add the grated cheese and leave it until it becomes cold. Grease a fireproof dish, and sprinkle it with cheese, and put tablespoonfuls of the semolina mixture all over it. They should stand up roughly like rock cakes ; bake to a golden brown in a fairly hot oven, which will take about twenty minutes.

Barley Rissoles

Ingredients.—¼lb. of pearl barley washed and soaked for twelve hours in cold water, ¼lb. of stock, seasoning, one gill of rather stiff white sauce. *Method.*—Bring to the boil and then simmer the pearl barley in the stock until it absorbs it, add salt and pepper—use either vegetable or bone stock, mix the cooked barley with a little white sauce made with flour (page 61) and the liquid the barley was simmered in, and more flavouring as required. Leave on a dish to cool. Form into rissoles, egg, crumb, and fry in a frying-basket in a stewpan of boiling fat until crisp and golden. Drain and serve hot. Add grated cheese if liked or serve plain with bacon for a breakfast dish. A seasoning of powdered herb may be added. If necessary bake instead of frying.

Savoury Barley Mould

Ingredients.—$\frac{1}{4}$lb. of washed pearl barley soaked for twelve hours, one and a half pint of stock, seasoning. *Method.*—Cook barley in the well-flavoured stock, adding more if required. Allow about two hours for this, first bringing to the boil and then simmer with the lid on. Season well with salt, pepper, powdered herb, if liked, add tiny dice of bacon. Press it well into a greased tin, mould and bake for a quarter of an hour in a hot oven, turn out and serve with sauce. It must be very hot. To save time and washing up the barley may be cooked in a casserole, baked and served in the casserole, and the sauce served separately.

Barley Stew

Ingredients.—½lb. pearl barley, two large onions, one head of celery, two leeks, one small carrot, one small turnip, a piece of cauliflower or white heart of cabbage, 1oz. of fat, pepper and salt, dumplings. *Method.* —Well wash and soak the barley for twelve hours. Put on to cook for three hours in a large casserole in two quarts of water. Melt the fat in a saucepan, cut the vegetables up finely and fry, then add the barley water and as much of the barley as desired to make the right consistency.

Simmer till the vegetables are tender ; half an hour before serving add the dumplings. More barley water or vegetable stock must be added if it gets too dry. After the vegetables are fried this can be put into a casserole to finish and be sent to table in the casserole.

Tapioca and Sago

are very starchy foods and are seldom used for savouries, but are valuable as bulk to add to soups or stews. The tapioca should be crushed and sprinkled into the soup or stew.

The small-seed sago does not need crushing. The large sago takes a long time to cook and so does the large tapioca. When used in soup in small quantities it should be boiled rather fast and only takes about ten minutes to cook. When used in puddings and stews it should be cooked gently and long.

A savoury sago or tapioca pudding may be made using part well-flavoured stock and part milk, allowing one pint to two ounces of sago, salt, pepper, and two ounces of grated cheese. Cook in a cool oven for two and a half to three hours.

Maize Porridge

Ingredients.—Four cups of water or milk, or part water and part milk, one and a quarter teaspoonfuls of salt, one cupful of mealie meal or more if the porridge is desired to be stiff. Put the salt into the milk, bring to the boil and stir in by degrees the meal. Cook for five minutes, then remove from the fire and cook at the back of stove for one hour, stirring occasionally in order to prevent it from burning. Serve with milk, butter and sugar, or syrup. Children who will not eat oatmeal porridge will often eat maize porridge.

Maize porridge, when cold, if cut into fingers, floured and fried, is good served with bacon—or grated cheese may be added to the maize mixture, which is then formed into balls, floured and fried, or baked.

Maize Meal Fritters

Ingredients.—Three cups of milk, two cups of best maize meal, one cup of flour, two eggs (beaten separately), half a teaspoonful of soda (dissolved in hot water), one teaspoonful of cream of tartar, one teaspoonful of salt, and half that quantity of pepper. *Method.* —Mix the dry ingredients together, then stir in the well-beaten yolks of the eggs and the soda dissolved in water and milk. Lastly, add the whites of eggs, beaten stiff, and mix well. Drop into boiling fat by the spoonful; when done drain over the pan so as not to waste any fat. Serve with tomato sauce.

Tinned Green Corn (Maize)

Ingredients.—One tin of corn, three table-spoonfuls of milk, ½oz. of fat, seasoning. *Method.*—Open the tin of corn and draw off the liquid, and then simmer the corn in the milk until tender, adding the fat, salt and pepper. The cooking takes about ten minutes.

Tinned Corn au Gratin

Ingredients.—Tin of corn prepared as above half a pint of white sauce, 2oz. of grated cheese, 1oz. of fine crumbs, seasoning. *Method.*—Grease a fireproof dish and sprinkle it with browned crumbs (this saves time in cooking afterwards), mix the corn and sauce and cheese and place in the dish and cover with browned crumbs. Bake about twenty minutes in a hot oven to brown.

Corn with tomato sauce, and corn with onion sauce is delicious served in the same fashion. Corn with poached or scrambled eggs is prepared as for tinned green corn and the eggs served on a bed of the corn.

Preparations of maize are Semola and Silver Flake. They taste much the same as semolina and are generally used in the same way for puddings.

VII
VEGETABLE DISHES

VII
VEGETABLE DISHES

TO COOK GREEN VEGETABLES SO THAT THEIR VALUE IS NOT LOST

ALL green vegetables—cabbage, brussels sprouts, turnip-tops, spring greens, peas, French beans, cauliflowers—are better and more wholesome if cooked by the conservative method. It preserves the mineral matter and natural sugar in the vegetables instead of allowing them to escape into the water, as is the case when boiling in a large quantity of water, and it retains the flavour, instead of drawing it out into the water.

Cabbage

Ingredients.—One cabbage, water, salt, soda. *Method.*—Trim and wash the cabbage, cut away all decayed leaves, put a saucepan of water on to boil, put in a teaspoonful of salt and a piece of soda the size of a pea. When the cabbage is ready, take half a gill of water out of the pan and put the cabbage into the pan; put on the lid and let it boil four or five minutes—not more. Strain off the water through a colander, put the half gill of water into the pan with half a tea-spoonful of salt, put in the cabbage, cover with the lid and simmer slowly till soft. Drain well and serve. It must simmer slowly or the small quantity of water will boil away and it will burn; it takes from half an hour to three-quarters according to the size of the vegetables. Instead of the water, after the vegetables have been blanched, if available two ounces of fat can be put into the pan and the cabbage is then put into it, the lid put on the saucepan, and it is simmered till tender. Instead of using a saucepan after the cabbage is blanched, the fat or small quantity of water is put into a casserole with the vegetables, the lid put on, and then it can be cooked either in the oven or on the range. A casserole must never be put directly over a fierce gas-jet.

All green vegetables should be cooked in this manner, but cauliflower is nice blanched in the above way, and then put into a steamer and steamed over boiling water.

Vegetable Soufflés

Ingredients.—4oz. vegetable purée (spinach, cabbage, sprouts, carrot, turnip, artichoke, tomato, celery, or several vegetables mixed, cooked, put through a sieve and flavoured), one gill of water, two eggs, 1oz. of flour, a pinch of salt. *Method.*—Put the butter and salt into a pan with the water. Stir, and when it boils sprinkle in the flour and stir briskly and cook until you have a paste. Add the purée (which should be rather dry) and stir. Remove from the fire and stir until mixed. Add the yolks of two eggs, one at a time, and then the frothed whites of two eggs. Bake in a greased soufflé-dish half full for ten minutes in a hot oven. This soufflé rises very much, and must be served the minute it is ready. The soufflé can be varied. For example, the remains of a dish of vegetable curry sieved and with some of the left-over rice added makes an excellent soufflé, or sieved vegetable and pearl barley (cooked) is delicious. An artichoke and pearl barley soufflé is specially attractive.

Cauliflower and Tomato Soufflé

Ingredients.—One cauliflower, three tomatoes, one gill white sauce, 1oz. grated cheese, whites of two eggs, salt, pepper, a few bread-crumbs. *Method.*—Boil or steam the cauliflower till soft, rub through a sieve with the tomatoes into a basin, add the white sauce and season. Whip the whites of egg to a stiff froth and stir lightly to the other ingredients, put into a buttered soufflé-mould, sprinkle a few bread-crumbs over, and bake in a fairly hot oven from twenty minutes to half an hour. Add the egg yolks to the sauce or use elsewhere.

Vegetable Pie

Ingredients.—Carrot, turnips, celery, beet-root, tomato, sprouts, French beans, etc. etc., seasoning, sauce. *Method.*—Use a mixture of cooked vegetables and divide them into small pieces. Warm them in brown tomato or curry sauce, season to taste. Fill a pie-dish with the sauce and vegetables, and cover with semolina or potato pastry (see pages 121 and 149). Bake in a quick oven for fifteen minutes.

Vegetable Irish Stew

Ingredients.—One teacupful of brown haricot beans, two teacupfuls of butter beans, 1½lb. of onions, 2lb. of potatoes, one carrot, one turnip, pepper and salt, 1oz. of fat, water. *Method.*—Soak and then cook the haricots in one quart of water to make the stock. Put the butter beans to soak overnight, and then cook in the same water in the morning in a large saucepan whilst the vegetables are being prepared. Slice the onions, peel the potatoes and leave whole. Cut up the carrots in thin slices, and the turnips in small pieces. Add all to the white beans, then add the haricot stock and seasoning. Cover closely, and stew for two hours. Make a round of pastry to about fit the size of the saucepan. Lay on the top of the stew and cook for half an hour longer. Cut into triangles, place the pastry round the dish and pour the stew in the centre. One hour before serving put in about twenty savoury dumplings and the seasoning. Let them cook gently.

An excellent winter dish.

Cauliflower Fritters (Hot)

Ingredients.—One cauliflower, some batter, fat, grated cheese, and coralline pepper. *Method.*—Cook the cauliflower, and break up into neat pieces. Dip these in frying batter until well covered, and then fry in boiling fat. Drain them well, and sprinkle with the grated cheese and pepper. Serve at once on a napkin. This is an excellent way of serving cauliflower which has been left over. Brussels sprouts are also delicious served as fritters. The cheese can be omitted, but makes the dish more nourishing.

Cabbage Stuffed with Rice

Ingredients.—One cabbage (with rather open leaves), one large onion, one cupful of bread-crumbs, a little chopped parsley, pepper and salt, one cupful of rice (cooked). *Method.*—Trim the outside of the cabbage and well wash without breaking the leaves. Cook the cabbage whole in a saucepan of boiling water for about fifteen minutes, drain in a colander. Slice and stew the onion, and mix with it the bread-crumbs, cooked rice, parsley, salt and pepper. Place some of this mixture between each leaf of the cabbage, tie the leaves together and put it into a casserole with a very little water. Cook slowly until quite tender.

Creamed Cabbage (Hot)

Ingredients.—One cabbage, 1oz. of fat, one gill milk, pepper and salt to taste. *Method.*—Boil the cabbage, drain it, cut it up small and put into a saucepan with the fat, milk, and seasoning of pepper and salt. Stir it all together over the fire until thoroughly hot, and serve in the casserole in which it was cooked.

Colcannon

Ingredients.—Some cold boiled potatoes, some cold boiled cabbage, some dripping, pepper and salt to taste. *Method.*—Take equal quantities of cold boiled potatoes and cold boiled cabbage. Mash the potatoes with a fork, chop the cabbage, mix together, place them in a saucepan or frying-pan with a little dripping, season with pepper and salt, and stir over the fire till the vegetables are hot and slightly browned. Grease a basin or pie-dish, put in the mixture, and bake in a hot oven for about half an hour, or, if liked, the vegetables may be served immediately after frying ; ½oz. to 1oz. of fat suffices for frying.

Mashed Swedes

Ingredients.—About 2lb. of swedes, 1oz. of fat, one tablespoonful of milk, a teaspoonful of salt, pepper, water to boil. *Method.*— Wash and peel the swedes, cut in quarters, or if very large into eight pieces each, put into a saucepan of boiling water to which a tea-spoonful of salt has been added. Boil till soft, drain, rub the turnips through a fine sieve, melt the fat in a saucepan, add the swedes and milk and seasoning. Make very hot. They can be put into a " gratin " dish, and have brown bread-crumbs sprinkled over them, be put into a hot oven, or under a griller and browned, thus making

Swede au Gratin

Carrots and turnips may be used in the same way.

Grated Carrots and Turnips

Wash and scrape and grate them. Place them in boiling salted water until soft (about twenty minutes for the carrot and ten minutes for the turnip, so that they must be cooked in separate pans). When soft drain well and serve as a vegetable or as a border to a mince or centre for cutlets, etc.

Onions and Tomatoes au Gratin

Ingredients.—Four large Spanish onions, six tomatoes, 1oz. of fine brown crumbs, seasoning. *Method.*—Peel the onions and put into boiling salted water and simmer for twenty to thirty minutes. Remove and cut into quarters. Cut the tomatoes into thick slices, grease a " gratin " dish and sprinkle with crumbs. Arrange the onion and tomato in it and season well and sprinkle with crumbs. Bake in a hottish oven for thirty minutes.

Stuffed Onions

Ingredients.—Six large onions (Spanish), 3oz. bread-crumbs, one teaspoonful of chopped parsley, half a teaspoonful of chopped sweet herbs, salt, pepper. *Method.*—Peel the onions, put them into cold water, bring to the boil and boil five minutes. Drain, and take out the centres, make a stuffing of the bread-crumbs, parsley, herbs, and mix with a beaten-up dried egg, season well and fill each onion with the mixture. Put side by side in a saucepan, pour in about one pint of brown gravy or stock, cover and simmer gently about four hours. Baste occasionally with the sauce. When tender, take them up carefully, thicken the gravy with a little flour or cornflour blended with cold water or stock, and poured into the hot stock; boil up again, season, pour over the onions and serve.

The onions can be stuffed with some minced meat mixed with a little gravy, parsley, and herbs, and cooked as above, or with any remains of cold ham or tongue or chicken. Or they can be stuffed with savoury rice (see recipe) and stewed in white sauce (see Sauces).

Spinach

Ingredients.—2lb. of spinach, 1oz. of fat, one tablespoonful of milk, small croûtons of fried bread. *Method.*—Wash the spinach very well in several waters and take away any decayed pieces. Put into a saucepan without water, over a very gentle heat, cover with the lid, and stir frequently till the water in the spinach oozes out. Add a teaspoonful of salt and a small piece of soda, and simmer till the spinach is tender. Drain and rub through a sieve, melt the fat in a saucepan, add the sieved spinach and make hot, then add the milk and seasoning. Add a dust of nutmeg if that flavouring is liked.

Spinach can be cooked in this manner and arranged in a flat bed, with poached eggs neatly laid on it or (dried) scrambled eggs arranged in the centre, and the spinach made into a border round. It can also be served piled on croûtons of bread and decorated with the hard-boiled yolk of an egg, rubbed through a sieve, and the white of the egg finely chopped. Turnip-tops and lettuce may be cooked like spinach.

Artichokes au Gratin (Jerusalem)

Ingredients.—2lb. of artichokes, half a pint of white sauce, 1oz. of fine brown crumbs, salt, pepper, anchovy sauce. *Method.*—Peel the artichokes and place in boiling salted water. Cook for twenty minutes, when they should be soft. Drain, slice, mix into the sauce, salt, pepper, and one tablespoonful of anchovy sauce. Add the artichokes, grease a soufflé or " gratin " dish. Put in the artichoke mixture. Cover with crumbs. Bake about twenty minutes in a fairly hot oven.

Chipped Artichokes

Ingredients.—2lb. of artichokes, salt, frying fat. *Method.*—Peel and slice the artichokes, dry them well in a clean cloth, place in a frying-basket and fry until brown and crisp. Drain well and scatter with salt and serve very hot. Do not peel long before they are needed and keep them covered or they will turn black. Potatoes are fried in the same way. For directions for frying see page 76.

Endive

The inner portion of the endive should be washed and made into salad, with oil and vinegar, pepper and salt. The outside leaves should be washed and cooked like spinach.

Braised Lettuce

Ingredients.—Six lettuces, one pint of vegetable stock, the yolk of an egg, one tablespoonful of milk, salt, pepper. *Method.* —Wash the lettuces, cut off the roots and any decayed leaves, and put them in a casserole with one pint of stock. Cover and cook in a moderate oven from thirty to forty minutes. Cut the lettuces in half, leave them in the casserole, sprinkle with salt and pepper, beat up the dried egg with the milk and add to the stock, stir till it thickens, but do not let it boil after the egg goes in or it will curdle.

Vegetable Marrow Fritters

Ingredients.—One vegetable marrow, 4oz. of flour, one tablespoonful of salad oil or 1oz. of fat, melted, one gill of tepid water, salt. *Method.*—Make a batter by putting the flour and salt into a basin, mix the salad oil or melted fat with the tepid water, make a well in the centre of the flour, add the water gradually, beat well and let it stand. Peel the marrow, cut into rounds about a quarter of an inch thick, remove the seeds, dip each round into the batter and fry in very hot fat.

Drain and serve on a dish-paper in a vegetable dish. Pieces of cooked marrow can be dipped into the batter and fried in the same way. The batter may be made without fat or oil if necessary.

Vol-au-Vent of Mushrooms, Peas, and Scrambled Eggs

Ingredients.—½lb. mushrooms, half a pint of peas, one pint of vegetable stock or milk, two eggs, salt, pepper, 1oz. of fat, 1oz. of flour. Fresh peas or Edgar's tinned marrowfats or Barr's dried marrowfat peas, cooked according to the directions on the packets, can be used for this, and savoury rice can be used in place of scrambled eggs. *Method.*—Stalk and peel the mushrooms, cut in dice and stew gently in the stock or milk, shell and boil the peas in the usual manner or cook the marrowfats according to directions, drain, and add to the mushrooms. When the latter are cooked, drain and keep the liquor. Melt the fat in a pan, add the flour, and blend well, add the liquor from the mushrooms, bring to the boil, stirring all the time and simmer five minutes ; add the vegetables and make hot. Add a squeeze of lemon-juice, season and put into the vol-au-vent pastry case, which of course will be made of plain pastry nowadays. Keep hot while the eggs are scrambled in the usual way and then lay the eggs on the top of the vegetables in the pastry case, and serve at once.

Scrambled Eggs

Ingredients.—Two or three eggs, two tablespoonfuls of milk, salt, pepper. *Method.*—Put the milk into a pan, break the eggs into a basin, and add to the other ingredients, season, put the pan over gentle heat and stir well all the time with a wooden spoon till the mixture thickens and looks rough, when it is ready. It must be stirred very vigorously when it begins to thicken.

Potato and Cabbage Cakes (Hot)

Ingredients.—Equal quantities of both cold potato and cabbage, one egg, white sauce, pepper and salt, a little flour. *Method.*—Mash the potato and cabbage smoothly together, adding beaten egg, white sauce, or melted butter to moisten. Flavour rather highly with pepper, add a little salt. Form

into round cakes, flour, and bake or fry.
Omit the egg if necessary.

Potato and Rice Cakes (Hot)

Ingredients.—Mashed potatoes, half the
quantity of boiled rice, a little fat, one egg,
a little flour, pepper, salt, and cayenne.
Method.—Take any remains of mashed potatoes and add half the quantity of boiled rice,
mix them all together with a little fat,
season well with pepper, salt, and a little
cayenne. Roll out on a floured board to
about an inch and a half thickness, cut into
rounds or squares with a cutter. Bake in
fast oven.

Potato and Egg Pie (Hot)

Ingredients.—Some cooked potatoes, egg
sauce (or onion purée), salt, pepper. *Method.*
—Mash the potatoes with plenty of egg sauce,
or use onion purée instead of egg sauce, and
flavour with salt and pepper. Place in a
fireproof china dish, and bake until lightly
browned.

Franklin's Potatoes

Ingredients.—Part-boiled potatoes, 2lb. ;
bread sauce, one pint. *Method.*—Take some

part-boiled potatoes and slice them. For this purpose waxy potatoes are best. Have ready some bread sauce and dilute it with a little more milk, so that it is a trifle thinner than the ordinary sauce. Put a layer in a soufflé-dish and then a layer of potatoes. Sprinkle with salt and pepper, finish with the sauce and a good sprinkling of fine bread-crumbs. Bake half an hour in a slow oven. If it does not brown nicely increase the heat at the last, or if you have a gas-cooker put it under the grill.

George Franklin's Potatoes

These are prepared as before, but soubise (onion) sauce is used instead of bread sauce.

Potato Mould

Ingredients.—1lb. of potatoes, 1lb. of carrots, about half a pint of milk and water. *Method.*—Boil the potatoes and carrots and well mash them. Pass through a fine wire sieve and mix all well together with the milk and water (warmed). Place in mould (which has been greased) and set in a hot oven for ten minutes. Turn out on a hot dish and brown in the oven. Serve with curry, tomato, or chutney sauce.

Stuffed Potatoes

Ingredients.—Six potatoes, seasoning, one gill of white onion sauce. *Method.*—Choose large potatoes all of a size and bake them. This takes about two hours in a moderate oven and the potatoes must be the same size, both for the look of the dish and because otherwise one would be over- and another under-done. When baked (this you can tell by putting in a skewer and if the potato is soft it is done) slice off a piece lengthways and scoop out the interior. Mix the potato with salt, pepper, and the sauce. Replace in the potato case and make thoroughly hot in the oven. The stuffing may of course be varied, using mince of meat or fish, stewed and sieved tomato, cheese sauce, shrimp sauce, mushroom sauce, or even just grated cheese and a little seasoning. A more elaborate-looking dish may be made by filling the potato and then piping a border of plain mashed potato round the edge.

Potato Curry

Cut cooked potatoes into cubes and serve hot in a curry sauce with boiled rice.

Potato and Nut Roll

Ingredients.—1lb. of mashed potatoes, 2oz. of ground nuts, one small onion finely minced, one teaspoonful of chopped parsley, one teaspoonful mixed herbs, 1oz. of fat, salt, pepper. *Method.*—Mix well, adding enough stock to bind, shape into a roll. Place on a greased tin and bake in a moderate oven until brown. Serve with any sauce such as curry, onion, or tomato.

Potato Pastry

Ingredients.—½lb. mashed potatoes, ½lb. flour, 3oz. fat, ½ teaspoonful baking powder, a little milk and water. *Method.*—Rub the fat into the flour, add the potatoes, salt, and baking powder. Mix to a stiff paste with milk and water. Roll out the paste to about ¼ inch in thickness on a floured board and use as required.

Vegetables au Gratin

Nearly all vegetables may be served " au gratin." Cold potatoes, flavoured with cheese or onion or sprinkled with nut, covered with white sauce and bread-crumbs, and baked, are excellent. Flageolets soaked or parboiled previously and placed in alternate layers in a fireproof dish with sliced tomato or potato sprinkled with onion make a valuable dish. Cold vegetables of any kind may be mixed with boiled rice and seasoned in an interesting manner. A layer of mashed potatoes, a sprinkling of bread-crumbs, and some knobs of fat complete the dish, which must be put into a hot oven so as to obtain a crisp brown top.

Curried Vegetables

The remains of cold vegetables are good curried and served up in a ring of rice, with fried croûtons placed upon them and with a few scalded sultanas set in small heaps upon the rice. Haricots and stoned prunes make a good curry, and slices of hard-boiled egg will eke out small quantities of cooked vegetables; in fact the vegetarian cook uses up all odds and ends in this way.

VIII
NUT DISHES

VIII
NUT DISHES

NUTS are a most valuable meat substitute—rich in protein and in fat. Many people who cannot eat them whole can digest them if put through a mincer. Nuts grated or chopped may be added to other dishes and are delicious in salads.

Nut Rolls

Ingredients.—1lb. cooked potatoes, 1lb. nuts of any kind, one egg, salt, pepper, cayenne. *Method.*—Mash the potatoes or rub them through a sieve, add enough milk to bind them. Put the nuts into boiling water to loosen the skins, and remove the skins; either chop them finely or put them through a mincing-machine or nut-mill. Mix them with the potato and season well. Beat up the egg and mix into the potato mixture, form into rolls, flour them well, put into a baking sheet with 1½oz. of dripping and bake in a fairly hot oven till brown, basting them well. Serve with a good brown or tomato sauce. If liked this can be made into one larger roll.

Nut Rissoles

Ingredients.—3oz. of rice, 4oz. of hazel nuts, 3oz. of pine kernels, one pint of milk or milk and water or vegetable stock, one egg, salt, pepper. *Method.*—Wash the rice and put it with the milk or stock into a double saucepan, and cook till the liquid is absorbed and the rice soft (about two hours). Remove the brown skin from the nuts and pine kernels and put through a mincing-machine. Beat up the yolk of the egg and add to the mixture, season well, and form into rissoles. Beat up the white of egg slightly, and dip the rissoles in, then roll in bread-crumbs and fry in hot fat. Drain well and serve on a dish-paper on a hot dish. Garnish with parsley.

A dried egg may be used, in which case yolk and white cannot be separated. If necessary bake the rissoles instead of frying.

Walnut Cutlets

Ingredients.—6oz. of shelled walnuts, 1lb. of bread-crumbs, one tablespoonful of flour, one gill of milk, ½oz. of fat, one lemon, one teaspoonful of grated onion, white of one egg. *Method.*—Make the bread-crumbs or put the bread through the mincing-machine with the walnuts. Melt the fat in a saucepan, add the flour, blend well, then add the milk, bring to the boil, stirring all the time, and boil about five minutes. Remove from the fire and add the bread-crumbs, walnuts, and grated onion, and a teaspoonful of lemon juice. Turn on to a plate to cool, then shape into cutlets, dip in milk or the slightly beaten white of egg, roll in crumbs and fry in hot fat. Serve with tomato or mushroom sauce.

Mushroom Sauce

Ingredients.—½lb. of mushrooms, one tablespoonful of flour, ½oz. of fat, one gill of milk. *Method.*—Peel and stalk the mushrooms, melt the fat in a pan, add the mushrooms finely chopped and fry about five minutes. Blend the flour smoothly with the milk, and stir into the mushrooms, bring to the boil, then simmer very gently about one hour. If they get too dry add more milk. Vegetable or cereal stock can be used in place of milk.

Chestnut Pie

Ingredients.—1lb. of chestnuts, 3oz. of macaroni, 1oz. of fat, 1oz. of flour, one pint of milk or the water the macaroni was boiled in (or half of each), salt, pepper. *Method.*— Boil the macaroni and strain. Put the chestnuts into boiling water and simmer half an hour, take them out of the water and skin them, chop them roughly, make a white sauce with the fat, flour, and milk, or water the macaroni was boiled in, add the chestnut and season well. Well grease a pie-dish, put in a layer of macaroni, then the chestnuts and sauce, then more macaroni. Cover with a nice short potato pastry and put into a fairly hot oven to bake.

Brussels Sprouts and Chestnuts

Ingredients.—1½lb. of sprouts, 1lb. of chestnuts, 2oz. of fat, water. *Method.*— Trim and clean the sprouts and soak in salted water about half an hour, drain and put into a saucepan of boiling water to which has been added one teaspoonful of salt and a piece of soda the size of a pea. Put the lid on the pan and boil for five minutes, drain, put the fat in a casserole, add the sprouts and the chestnuts after preparing them as follows : Put them into boiling water and simmer half an hour, then remove the skins and put them into the casserole with the sprouts, sprinkle salt and pepper over, put on the lid and cook gently on the range, or in the oven, till both are tender. Serve in the casserole. Be careful not to let them cook too fast in the casserole or they will burn.

Nut Salad

Ingredients.—Half a cooked beetroot, the best portions of a head of celery (use the remainder stewed or for soup), ½lb. of nuts, sauce. *Method.*—Slice the beetroot and arrange on it the shelled, skinned and chopped nuts and shred celery. Dress with salad dressing made with unsweetened condensed milk, lemon juice, salt and pepper.

A Nut Savoury

Ingredients.—Half a rasher of bacon and one stewed prune per head, chopped nuts. *Method.*—Remove the stones from the stewed prunes and stuff with nuts. Roll each in bacon and tie. Cook on a tin in a fairly hot oven for ten to fifteen minutes just to cook the bacon. Serve very hot on little strips of toasted bread. Remove the string before serving.

IX
CHEESE DISHES

IX

CHEESE DISHES

CHEESE is extremely nourishing, having a higher percentage of protein and of fat even than meat.

Those persons who formerly found it indigestible when eaten with meat may find themselves able to eat it in company with meatless foods, and persons of delicate digestion can partake of it when grated though they cannot do so in any other way. Grated and served between bread and butter it is a nourishing food for children.

Welsh Rarebit

Ingredients.—1½oz. of cheese, 1oz. of clarified fat, pepper and salt, half a teaspoonful of made mustard, a square of toast. *Method.*—Grate or cut up the cheese small, put it in a saucepan with the fat, pepper, salt, and mustard. Stir for a few minutes till the mixture is thick and soft. Pour over the buttered toast and serve very hot.

Cheese and Potato Pie

Ingredients.—2lb. of potatoes, one egg (boiled hard), 1oz. of grated cheese, ½oz. of fat, 1oz. of flour, three-quarters of a pint of milk, salt, pepper. *Method.*—Boil the potatoes till nearly soft, drain them and cut into slices. Cut the egg into slices, and make a sauce with the fat, flour, and milk as in macaroni cheese, and add half the cheese to it, season. Grease a pie-dish, put in layers of potato, egg, and sauce, finishing with sauce. Sprinkle with the rest of the cheese, and some brown bread-crumbs, and bake in a quick oven about ten minutes.

Cheese Pasties

Ingredients.—1oz. of cheese, 2oz. of bread-crumbs, ½oz. of fat, one teaspoonful of made mustard, half a teaspoonful of salt, quarter of a teaspoonful of pepper, short crust pastry. *Method.*—Make some short crust pastry, according to the recipe for beefsteak pie, roll it out thin and cut into rounds with a large round cutter or the top of a tumbler. Cut the cheese into very small dice, add the bread-crumbs, melted fat, mustard, salt and pepper, mix well, lay a spoonful of the mixture on one side of the pastry rounds, brush the edges with water, fold the other side over, press well together, put on a greased baking-sheet and bake in a hot oven for about fifteen minutes. Potato pastry may be used instead of flour pastry.

Macaroni Cheese

Although this is such a well-known dish it is so often badly made that it may be as well to insert a recipe.

Ingredients.—3oz. of cooked macaroni, 1½oz. of cheese, 1oz. of fat, 1oz. of flour, one teaspoonful of made mustard, one pint of milk or half milk and half water the macaroni was cooked in, salt, pepper. *Method.*—Boil the macaroni, grate the cheese, melt the fat in a saucepan, add the flour and mustard, cook two or three minutes without browning, remove the pan from the fire, and stir the milk gradually to the mixture, mixing well so that it is free from lumps, return the pan to the fire, bring to the boil, stirring all the time, let it simmer five minutes then add the macaroni and three-quarters of the cheese and seasoning, let it get hot then turn it into a greased pie-dish or fireproof dish, sprinkle the remaining cheese over the top. Brown under a griller or in a hot oven. Send to table in the dish it is cooked in. Rice can be cooked in the same way.

Tomato Cheese Croûtons

Ingredients.—½lb. of tomatoes, one onion (small), one rasher of bacon or 1oz. of cooked ham, one teaspoonful mixed herbs (tied in muslin), some parsley stalks, 1oz. of grated cheese, one tablespoonful of milk, salt, pepper, croûtons of bread, 1oz. of fat. *Method.*— Slice the tomatoes, shred the onion, finely cut up the bacon or ham into small pieces. Melt the fat in a saucepan, put in the tomatoes, bacon, onion, herbs, and parsley and cook gently till tender. Rub through a sieve, add the milk, return to the pan, and add the grated cheese. Put a little on each croûton of bread, serve very hot. A little chopped parsley sprinkled over each is an improvement. To make the croûtons, cut some bread about a quarter of an inch thick, cut it into rounds and fry in hot fat. If fat cannot be spared use toast or hot biscuits.

Potato and Cheese Soufflés (Plain)

Ingredients.—½lb. of cooked potatoes, 2oz. of grated cheese, half a gill of milk, salt, pepper. *Method.*—Rub the potatoes through a sieve, return them to the saucepan, add the milk and half the cheese and seasoning, make hot, put into a greased soufflé-dish or small ramekin cases, sprinkle the rest of the cheese over the top and bake in a fairly quick oven about ten minutes.

Savoury Cheese Pancakes (Hot)

Ingredients.—¼lb. of flour, two dried eggs, half a pint of milk and water, half a table-spoonful of grated cheese, a pinch of mixed herbs, quarter of a teaspoonful of baking-powder, pinch of salt and cayenne, a little dripping. *Method.*—Put the flour into a basin, adding the pinch of salt and cayenne, whisk the eggs and pour them gradually into the flour, mixing it well with a wooden spoon, then add by degrees the milk, working the batter until it is perfectly smooth, cover the basin with a cloth and let the batter stand for an hour if possible. Just before using it stir into it the grated cheese, mixed herbs, and baking-powder. Put a small omelette-pan on the stove (where the heat is steady) with a piece of dripping in it; when the fat is boiling, add sufficient of the batter to cover the pan evenly, and when the under-side is lightly browned shake the pan and turn the pancake, and directly it is evenly browned on the other side remove it from the pan and place it on paper and roll it up. Serve with a hot sauce.

Cheese Custard Pudding (Hot)

Ingredients.—3oz. of cheese, two cupfuls of milk, two eggs, 2oz. of fine, stale bread-crumbs. *Method.*—Beat all well together, and bake for about half an hour in a fire-proof dish in not too hot an oven.

Potted Cheese

Ingredients.—Odds and ends of cheese, fat, made mustard, salt, pepper, cayenne. *Method.*—Take any pieces of cheese and grate them and then work to a smooth paste with the other ingredients, using enough fat to make the paste smooth. Press into an earthenware tureen with a cover. Excellent with hot biscuits or toast or to use as sandwiches. About a quarter the quantity of lentil purée may be added to the cheese.

Milk Cheese (to make at home)

Ingredients.—Milk, salt. *Method.*—Let 1 or 2 quarts of milk stand for three or more days until thick. Fasten some butter muslin over a basin, pour the curd on to it, and mash with a fork. Tie the muslin together to form a bag, and hang up with a basin under. Next day untie and fold the curd flat inside the muslin, place on a sieve and let it drain. Turn now and then and break up the curd with a fork. When firm beat in a little salt and press into a neat shape. Use the whey for mixing scones, cakes, etc., instead of milk.

X
WAR ECONOMY BREADS AND SCONES

X

WAR ECONOMY BREADS AND SCONES

Barley-Meal and Wheatmeal Bread

Ingredients.—1¾lb. seconds flour, 1¾lb. barley-meal, 1oz. yeast (compressed), one small tablespoonful salt, one and three-quarters to two pints lukewarm water. *Method.*—Warm two basins. Into one put the flour and salt and barley-meal, mix well and stand in a warm place. Put the yeast into the other and work with a wooden spoon till liquid with the tepid water. Make a well in the middle of the flour, strain in the yeast and water, sprinkle a little flour from the sides over the top, cover with a thick cloth, and stand in a warm place for about half an hour, till the water and yeast have bubbles on the top. This is called setting the sponge. Take up the basin and mix all together, adding more tepid water if required, until the dough is soft; turn on to a floured board and knead well until smooth; flour the basin, put the dough back into it, cut a cross on the top with the back of a knife, cover, and stand in a warm place for two hours. Then knead, shape into loaves, put into greased, floured tins, which should be warm, and stand the tins in a warm place about twenty minutes to prove. The tins should only be half full when the dough is put in, and it should rise to the top. Put into a hot oven for about fifteen minutes and then move to a cooler part, and bake from fifty minutes to an hour. Small loaves take from thirty-five to forty-five minutes, and when cooked the bread should give a hollow sound when tapped.

Maize-Meal and Wheatmeal Bread

Ingredients.—1½lb. standard flour, ¾lb. maize-meal, about half a pint tepid water or milk and water mixed, ¼oz. yeast, quarter of a teaspoonful of sugar, one teaspoonful of salt. *Method.*—Mix the flour, maize-meal, and salt in a warm basin and warm slightly in front of the fire. Cream the yeast till liquid with the tepid water; make a well in the centre of the flour, pour in the yeast and water, sprinkle over flour from the sides, cover the basin, and put in a warm place to rise for about an hour. Take it up, mix into a dough, knead it well and put it back into the basin, cover, and set to rise again in a warm place about one hour. Knead again, form into loaves, and put into greased tins. Set them in a warm place to rise about half an hour, prick the top with a fork, and bake in a hot oven thirty to forty minutes, according to the size of the loaves.

If cottage loaves are liked, take two pieces of dough—one only one-third the size of the other—form into balls, put the smaller one on the larger, and push the forefinger into the middle on the top. Make two or three cuts round the sides, place on a floured tin, set to prove, then bake like the tin loaves, only allowing about a quarter of an hour longer.

Wheatmeal and Rice Bread

Ingredients.—1½lb. standard flour, ¾lb. cooked rice, half a pint rice water (tepid),

¼oz. yeast, one teaspoonful of salt. *Method.* —Boil the rice (2oz. of which yield ¼lb. when cooked) in one quart of salted water. Drain and beat it to a paste; add it to the flour, when warm, together with the salt, mix well; cream the yeast with the tepid rice water, and mix all well together into a dough. Set to rise in a warm place two to three hours; take it up and knead well, adding a little more flour if necessary; form into loaves, put into greased tins, set to rise half an hour, or till the dough rises to the top of the tins, bake in a hot oven thirty to forty minutes.

Note.—The rice must be well boiled, and if the rice water is too thick it can be thinned down with tepid water.

In all kinds of bread, if the dough is too dry when ready for kneading, a little tepid water can be added, and the rules for keeping everything warm and out of draughts, and the heat of the oven, are the same for all.

Wheatmeal and Oatmeal Bread

Ingredients.—1½lb. standard flour, ¾lb. cooked oatmeal, half a pint tepid water,

¼oz. yeast, one teaspoonful of salt. *Method.*
—Boil 2oz. of oatmeal till soft in the usual
way. Drain well, then make the bread
according to the directions for rice bread.

Ryemeal and Wheatmeal Bread

This can be made in the same proportions
as the barley-meal and wheatmeal bread,
and in the same manner.

Points to Remember

Be sure to have the basins warm.

Use lukewarm water about 70° to mix.

Cover the basin well and keep in a warm
place free from draughts when setting the
sponge and proving the dough. If in too
hot a place the bread will be sour, if too
cold it will not rise.

Bread requires a hot oven at first to kill
the yeast and stop it rising further, or the
loaf will be full of holes. The proper heat
is 400°.

For Potato Bread see page 183.

SCONES MADE FROM WHEAT MIXED WITH OTHER CEREALS

Maize-Meal and Wheatmeal Scones

Ingredients.—1lb. maize-meal, 1lb. flour, one teaspoonful carbonate of soda, one teaspoonful cream of tartar, half a teaspoonful salt, one tablespoonful syrup or treacle, about one pint buttermilk or sour milk. Fresh milk can be used or half milk and half water, but buttermilk or sour milk makes a very light scone. *Method.*—Put the flour and maize-meal, soda, and cream of tartar into a basin and mix well together. Make a well in the centre of the flour and pour in enough milk to make a soft dough. It is difficult to say the exact quantity of moisture required as some flour takes more than others. Flour a board and rolling-pin, turn the dough on to it, divide in pieces and roll each piece into a round about a quarter of an inch thick, cut each piece into four, and bake on a greased girdle over not too hot a fire. If liked, it can be rolled out in one piece about a quarter of an inch thick and cut into rounds with a cutter or the top of a tumbler.

Potato Scones or Cakes

Ingredients.—1lb. cold boiled potatoes, ¼lb. flour, 1oz. dripping, salt, about one table-spoonful milk. *Method.*—Rub the potatoes through a fine sieve and add the flour and salt. Melt the dripping, add the milk to it, and warm slightly, add to the potato mixture and mix well together. Turn on to a floured board and roll out about half an inch thick. Cut into rounds and bake on a greased girdle over a moderate heat. When brown on one side, turn over. They can be put on a greased tin and baked in a hot oven about ten minutes. If you have no girdle a thick frying-pan can be used.

Barley-Meal Scones

Ingredients.—1lb. barley-meal, half a small teaspoonful carbonate of soda, one teaspoonful cream of tartar, half a teaspoonful salt, about half a pint milk, buttermilk or sour milk. *Method.*—Sieve the carbonate of soda and the cream of tartar into the barley-meal, add the salt, and mix well. Add enough milk to make a soft dough. Rub a

M

little barley-meal on to a board, turn the dough on to it, divide into three, roll out each piece about a quarter of an inch thick cut into four, and bake on a greased girdle over a moderate heat or in a fairly hot oven on a greased baking-sheet. If liked, this can be all rolled out at once and cut into rounds.

Another way of making these scones is to put ½lb. of barley-meal into a bowl, add a pinch of salt, stir in enough cold water to make a fairly stiff dough, roll out on a floured board, cut into rounds about a quarter of an inch thick, and bake on a greased girdle or thick frying-pan. When one side is brown turn to the other, split them open, spread with margarine, and serve hot.

Yet another way is to put 1lb. of barley-meal into a basin with a pinch of salt, melt 1oz. of fat, add half a pint of warm milk, and stir into the meal. If too moist add a little more meal, if too dry a little more warm milk. Cook on a greased girdle.

Rice Scones

Ingredients.—1lb. rice, one teaspoonful sugar, one teaspoonful salt, one quart water,

¼lb. flour. *Method.*—Put the water, rice, sugar, and salt into a saucepan, bring to the boil, then let simmer slowly till the rice has become soft and has absorbed the water. Put the flour on a board and turn the rice on to it. When cool enough to handle mix into the flour, roll out thin, and cut into rounds. Bake either on a greased and floured girdle over a moderate fire or on a greased baking-sheet in a hot oven about a quarter of an hour.

Oatmeal Biscuits

Ingredients.—3oz. medium oatmeal, 3oz. flour, 2oz. of fat, half a teaspoonful of carbonate of soda, pinch of salt, 1oz. sugar, one dried egg. *Method.*—Mix the oatmeal and flour, carbonate of soda, salt, and sugar together, rub in the fat. Beat up the egg with one tablespoonful of water and add. Mix to a stiff dough, roll out about a quarter of an inch or less thick on a floured board, cut into rounds, and bake on a greased baking-sheet in a moderate oven for a quarter of an hour. The egg can be omitted and milk and water used instead.

Oat Cakes

Ingredients.—4oz. medium oatmeal, 1½oz. flour, 1oz. of fat, quarter of a teaspoonful carbonate of soda, quarter of a teaspoonful cream of tartar, one teaspoonful sugar, half teaspoonful salt, about two tablespoonfuls milk. *Method.*—Mix the oatmeal, flour, carbonate of soda, cream of tartar, salt, and sugar together, and rub in the fat, add the milk, and mix to a stiff paste. Divide into four pieces, roll each piece to a thin round, and bake on a greased baking-sheet in a moderate oven about a quarter of an hour.

Johnny Cake

Ingredients.—1lb. maize-meal, about half a pint of water, half teaspoonful of salt. *Method.*—Put the meal and salt into a basin, add the water, and mix and beat well. Make into a thin cake, put on a greased baking-sheet in a hot oven.

Maize-Meal and Flour Baking-Powder Rolls

Ingredients.—¾lb. flour, ¼lb. maize-meal, one teaspoonful salt, two teaspoonfuls baking-powder, about half a pint milk or milk and water. *Method.*—Mix the flour, maize-meal, baking-powder, and salt well together in a basin. Make a well in the centre, add the milk, and mix all to a rather soft dough. Shape into rolls, and bake at once in a fairly hot oven.

Points to Remember

(1) Do not add all the moisture to the above recipes at once in case they are too moist. If too dry, add a little more liquid than the recipe gives.

(2) Always cook anything which contains carbonate of soda or baking-powder as soon as possible after the moisture is added, therefore have girdle or baking-sheet and oven ready before mixing.

(3) Have a clear fire under the girdle, but not too fierce or it will burn the scones. If cooked over a gas-jet do not turn it full on, but remember to grease the girdle and make it hot before putting the scones on to it.

(4) Turn all cakes cooked on a girdle or frying-pan when a light brown on one side, and then brown on the other.

Yeast (Home-made)

Put 2 quarts of water into a saucepan and add ¼oz. of hops, two potatoes, sliced, one tablespoonful of moist sugar or malt; boil twenty minutes, then strain it through a sieve; let it stand till it has cooled to about 90 degrees, or the heat of new milk, then add ½oz. of baker's or compressed yeast. Pour all into a deep jar or jug, to allow it to ferment without running over, and allow it to rise and fall once before being used. Keep a small quantity of this yeast in a bottle to use, instead of baker's yeast, the next time you wish to make it. It will keep in a cool place about two months. This quantity of yeast is sufficient for a stone of flour, keeping out a pint in a bottle for using to quicken the next yeast made, in place of baker's yeast.

Another method of making yeast is to put a handful of hops into a quart of cold water; bring it to the boil and boil for twenty minutes. Put two tablespoonfuls of barley or rye flour, one of salt, and one of moist sugar, into a basin and mix well; strain the hop liquor on to it, and stir well. When about the heat of new milk, stir in one gill of brewer's yeast. Let it stand in a cool place for twenty-four hours, then bottle for use. When a fresh supply of yeast is needed, one pint of this yeast can be used to ferment it with in place of brewer's yeast. Do not forget to stir this yeast before using it, and in cold weather keep it in a warm place. When making bread with this it is best to set the sponge overnight, and after the dough is kneaded it takes about two hours to rise.

About one and a quarter gills of this yeast are required to raise 1 stone or 14lb. of flour.

Yeast is not easy to make, and needs practice and great care in obtaining the right temperature.

Potato Bread

Bread made with Flour and 25 per cent. Potato

Ingredients.—7lb. of flour, 2lb. 5½oz. of potatoes, 2oz. of yeast, 1oz. of salt, 2½ pints of water. *Method.*—Mix the flour and salt together and warm slightly. Scrub the potatoes, steam, then peel, and sieve them while still hot. Mix the potatoes, flour, and salt together.   Cream the yeast with a little of the water.   Pour this into the centre of the flour, and work the whole into a dough, adding the remainder of the water gradually. Set to rise in a warm place, covered with a damp cloth for about two hours.   Remove from the basin and knead thoroughly. Divide the dough into even-sized pieces, shape into loaves, and put each into a greased tin, or on to a floured baking sheet.   Put in a warm place to rise for another fifteen minutes, and then bake in a hot oven for about forty-five minutes.

Note.—The amount of liquid greatly depends on the kind of potatoes used ; $1\frac{1}{2}$oz. of yeast would be sufficient if a longer time could be allowed for rising.

This recipe is provided by the Ministry of Food.

XI

THE ECONOMICAL USE
OF SUGAR

IT is certainly true that cheapness and a
plentiful supply have given us all the oppor-
tunity of using sugar in a very lavish manner,
but the retrenchment is not altogether loss,
for many people find that their food digests
better when less sugar is used in cookery.

The use of very much sweetened dishes is
purely a habit, and I therefore suggest a
method of breaking it which has commended
itself to various people :

(1) Train your taste to desire less sugar.
Begin by using just a quarter less than you
are accustomed to use in every recipe, in a
week use half as much, and soon you will be
quite content with the lessened quantity.

(2) In order to economize sugar, when
using rough " black " sugar, make it into
syrup with boiling water, strain it to remove

dirt, and use it in tea, coffee, and for puddings, etc., in the form of syrup. Indeed,
sugar syrup might always be used in tea
and coffee, as often the sugar put into the
cup does not entirely dissolve, and so a
considerable proportion of it is wasted. This,
occurring as it does in a country numbering
some forty-five million people, accounts for
a great wastage of a valuable food.

(3) When stewing sour fruit add half a
teaspoonful of bicarbonate of soda to each
pound of fruit. This neutralizes the acid,
and thus less sugar is needed.

(4) When making marmalade and jam use
part glucose. It is no cheaper than sugar, but
the point is that it is often obtainable when
sugar is not.   It is used in the same way as
sugar. The best result is obtained from a
mixture of two parts sugar to one part glucose,
but half sugar and half glucose is satisfactory.

Glucose is made of starch, chiefly obtained
from maize. A great authority says re-
garding it : " Those persons who dislike the
idea of using it should remember that starchy
foods, in course of digestion acted on by the
acids in the human body, form sugar."
Therefore we are practically manufacturing
glucose inside us almost hourly.

Saccharine may be used for tea, coffee, and sweetening stewed fruit; half a grain to a breakfast-cup of tea is sufficient.

In the country, where honey may be procured, many people use it to sweeten light puddings, and a little stirred into fruit salad gives a very delicious flavour. The whole question for adults reduces itself, as I have said, to habit, whereas for children and growing boys and girls sugar is almost a necessity.

The Use of Sugar Beet

Many people have grown sugar beet and are at a loss now to know how to use it other than as food for animals. The following method produces a palatable syrup which can be used for sweetening puddings and tarts, and so make it possible to save out of the sugar ration in order to have some sugar for jam making :

Wash and peel the beet and put it into a large fireproof jar till half full, then fill it up with cold water and put it into a moderate oven and leave it in all day and all night, taking it out next morning before the fire is lit. Strain off the juice, and to every pint add one large tablespoonful of glucose. Put the juice and glucose on a hot fire and stir until melted and then boil fast until it thickens (about half an hour). The resulting syrup is a light brown colour with a pleasant flavour and delicious when a little was added to stewed fruit, boiled puddings, or porridge, at the time of eating them.

The sugar beet after the syrup has been extracted can be used for fritters served with brown gravy or white sauce, chopped and fried like fried potatoes, seasoned with pepper and salt and a little chopped parsley. Sugar beet contains so much moisture that it needs longer frying than potatoes.

Puddings

Note.—Puddings and sweets are not included here as quantities of recipes may be found in almost any cookery-book, but it is useful to know that one-third to one-half barley, rice, maize-flour, fine oatmeal or mashed potato may be mixed with wheat-flour in pastry and puddings, and that the amount of fat advised may generally be halved. The less fat used the more liquid will be needed.

INDEX

Lightning Source UK Ltd.
Milton Keynes UK
UKHW03f0625060718
325319UK00007B/350/P

9 781278 730752